Miracles Along
THE
PATH

My Personal Accounts
Spanning 50 years

Appreciation

Thank you, Don, Susan, Joy, and Beverly for helping me get this witness of God's love and close attention to the details of our daily lives ready to share with others. Thank you for your objective suggestions that helped clarify my perspective. I thank God for all of you. I give thanks and praise to Jesus for giving us the Holy Spirit to inspire and guide us to do the Father's will.

Dedication

To my best friend, whom I have been close to as far back as I can remember......JESUS.

To my parents, Austin and Matilda, for their unconditional love and nurturing faith in God by word and example.

To my husband, Hans, whom I cherish deeply for his loving tenderness, partnership, patience, and support.

To my stepson, Curt, whom I had the privilege to help raise. He has brought me much joy and happiness.

To my precious brothers and sisters, whom I love dearly and who encouraged me to continue in this endeavor. Each one holds a special place in my heart.

Table of Contents

Introduction

One day during prayer, the thought of writing down some of the miracles in my life popped into my head, but immediately I realized what a big undertaking that would be and discounted it. From time to time, this became a recurring thought. I did nothing about it though.

Several months had passed when I began getting strong promptings from the Holy Spirit. First, an evangelist spoke on being obedient to the leading of the Spirit, taking steps to obey what persists in our hearts. Then, one day while reading my Bible, Matt. 7:24, 26 jumped out at me: "All who listen to My instructions and follow them are wise, like a man who builds his house on solid rock....but those who hear My instructions and ignore them are foolish." During prayer another day, Luke 9:62 stood out: "Anyone who lets himself be distracted from the work I plan for him is **not fit** for the Kingdom of God." That did it! I said, *"OK, Lord."*

Little by little, the Lord began reminding me of the miracles in my life, so I started jotting them down in the back of my Bible. I was surprised to eventually see how many there were. After prayer time or sometimes while watching television, the prompting would be so evident, the desire so strong that I would turn the set off, get the notebook and just pray, *"Lord, I am willing, but You have to do it."* I would look in the back of my Bible, pick the earliest miracle I recalled, and eventually wrote them in the sequence in which they occurred. The title would be scripted and the words would just flow. The Lord told the miracle accounts for me! I was always astonished to realize that I was not straining to remember the facts or details, but that the Holy Spirit was enlightening me to recount these miracles. It truly felt as if the words were coming out of the end of my pencil as I recalled so vividly the events just as they happened. *"Thank You for using me, Lord Jesus,"* I prayed.

What Exactly Is a Miracle?

World Book Dictionary defines a miracle :

"...a wonderful happening that is contrary to

or independent of the known laws of nature."

A Christian definition :

...a supernatural phenomenon, which comes

about most often because of one's faith and

trust in God, where there is no evidence or

proof of origin.

Psalm 23: 1-4

"The Lord is my shepherd.

He maketh me to lie down

in green pastures,

He leads me beside the still waters.

He restores my soul;

He leads me in the paths of

righteousness

For His name's sake.

Yea though I walk through the valley

of the shadow of death,

I will fear no evil

For You are with me;

Your rod and Your staff,

they comfort me."

My First Miracle

CHAPTER 1

I was eight years old born in the middle of four brothers and two sisters, ranging in age from twenty down to two years of age. I already had a deep-rooted faith in God because my parents were a tremendous example to follow in my relationship with Him. My daddy was a well-respected, honorable man. He taught his children strength of character, integrity, and honesty. My mother was a devout Christian. She had the ability to make everyone feel special, but without the exclusion of anyone else's specialness.

We are a Catholic family; we prayed together often. I heard my mother and daddy speak about Novenas and I knew they were prayed for a certain amount of time. For instance, one could go to Mass for nine days in a row for a special need or pray a given prayer for nine consecutive hours, etc. Much as with fasting, the idea was not the mechanics of it, but the heartfelt sacrifice offered to God. Whatever you wanted to give up or do extra as an offering to God for your special need was fine. The point during that time was to die to self and put your focus more on the Lord.

At forty-six years old, my daddy had already suffered three heart attacks and could not work or even go upstairs anymore. He spent much of his time reading and, in fact, read the entire Bible during this time. My mother must have felt something. Later, we realized that it was a prompting from the Holy Spirit because she decided to start a nine day Novena that Daddy would get well and I will never forget her words to the Lord, **"Thy will be done."** She fervently completed the nine days and my precious daddy died on the evening of the **ninth day.** As a result of the Holy Spirit's guidance and Mother's obedience, we had **peace beyond understanding.** Because he died at the end of the ninth day, we had received an obvious sign from Heaven that this was indeed God's will. We cried, we missed him, and still do, but we had tremendous **peace** knowing that the Lord heard and answered Mother's prayers personally by the answer coming at the precise ending of the Novena. This was for me a never-to-be-forgotten message of the Lord's miraculous closeness to our every need and prayer.

The following poem was found in Daddy's desk after his death. Our uncle, who is a Catholic priest, asked one of the monks, a calligrapher, to hand print it beautifully for all of us and we have it framed in our homes. This poem has given each of us continued guidance from our daddy all these years.

To **EACH** of MY **FAMILY**

"By night or by day, when loved ones are thousands
of miles away,

if you remain Pure, **Honest**, and True, take heart and
don't be blue.

For we will sit down together again and talk just like we
used to do,

in even our new Home in Heaven, where we shall be
forever happy and forever together."

Daddy
By: James Austin Hunt

A Child in Pain

CHAPTER 2

From the time I was two, my sweet mother had to take care of me as I cried in pain from almost constant earaches. The doctor discovered a hole in my eardrum for which there was no cure. My ear would run a smelly fluid, so I kept cotton in it all of the time. Mother was instructed to syringe it out with water daily and to put medicated ear drops in my ear several times a day. At times, the pain was excruciating, and I made many trips to the ear doctor from two years until fourteen years old. My precious loving mother never showed signs of impatience or complained, not once. With raising four boys, she must have been weary of this additional chore.

Years later, when I was fourteen, a new doctor we had been seeing suggested we try an experimental surgical procedure. It was to graft skin from behind my ear to close the hole. We were very happy to try it. My prayer to Jesus was very simple: "*Dear Jesus, please let this operation work, and don't let me ever have ear trouble again. If You do this for me, I will thank you every day for the rest of my life*". Well, the surgery was definitely a success—no more earaches, no more fluid running out.

For two years, I continued thanking Jesus every day. A retreat came up at the Academy of the Immaculate Conception, where I attended the first two years of high school. During one of the conferences, the priest was speaking about praying and talking to God. Then all of a sudden, I heard him say, as if God were saying it directly to me loud and clear, "If there is something you are thanking God for, He heard you and you do not have to keep saying it anymore." I remember my heart pounding; I knew this message was for me, probably others too.

As a child, when I prayed to Jesus, I felt that He was my best friend who loved me in spite of all my faults and sins. I felt so loved, protected, and warm when talking to Him. I loved to go to Mass every day, even in summer. I would make a short visit to church during recess, or after school, or sometimes after girl scouts, or volleyball practice. I loved being in His presence. The awesome reality of Jesus' loving tenderness is a tremendous miracle still today.

Psalm 121: 1-2

"I will lift up my eyes to the hills,

From whence comes my help.

My help comes from the Lord,

Who made heaven and earth."

The Convent Experience

CHAPTER 3

Etched in my memory, as early as eight years old, are those times I knelt beside my bed at night praying for each individual in my family and just talking to Jesus. I prayed that my vocation would be to become a Catholic nun. I wanted to be as close to Jesus on this earth as I possibly could, and I felt this was a sure fire way to get to Heaven. This I wanted more than anything.

After eighth grade, in the fall of 1961, I went to an academy that was located on the same hill as the Convent of the Immaculate Conception. I loved it there. I certainly was not an angel there, but then I never was. I knew all my young years that I was going to become a nun, so I decided to come home for my junior and senior years to have some fun dating. Then, I knew I was going to enter the convent upon graduation.

During the spring and summer after graduation, I dated a gorgeous young man whom I grew to really care about. He started going to church with me and we had a lot of fun together. I didn't tell him, until one month before I was to leave for the convent, that I was going. I'm not proud to say, he was devastated because he had just asked me to marry him. However, I have to tell you, I really felt I gave him up for Jesus. It was very tempting to follow my feelings for him, but Jesus had a much deeper place in my heart.

It was August of 1965. What an exciting day experiencing ten years of prayers being answered! The convent was a great life; I loved it. We, of course, had certain times of the day that we prayed together, and the life was just what I expected. I loved the other sisters. We had lots of fun and we were growing into dedicated women. I had been there two years, and as usual, one day we went to church for prayer. Never will I forget what happened next. I knelt down to pray and **no one was there!** My words, my prayers were bouncing back at me, as if hitting a wall. I bet I turned white as a sheet; I was stunned. Never, in my whole life had I felt this. Continuing in prayer, I hoped this was my imagination or something other than what I suspected—Jesus had withdrawn from me for some reason.

Immediately, my mind began trying to figure out what could have caused this. You see, I recognized what this absence was because, over the years, I have had many opportunities to share my faith, what it means to me, and how the Lord works in my daily life. I've heard at times from others, "I wish I had your faith. When I pray, it's like praying to a wall." For the first time, I knew what that felt like, what they were talking about. It was devastating to me.

I'm sure that I asked Jesus what to do. But the only

thing I remember clearly after that happened was that I sat there in church in shock for awhile and then made a decision which I have never questioned and never felt bad about, or regretted in all the now thirty-nine years later. Even though I was happy in the convent, I could only conclude that the Lord, my Lord, was telling me to leave, that He had another plan for my life. Maybe, since I prayed to be a nun from the time I was a little girl, He had given me the desire of my heart, but now He needed me somewhere else. For what other reason would my Lord allow something so blatantly devastating to happen to me? This separation from God was without a doubt, the worst period of my entire life.

It was September of 1967, a little into my third year, after I had just taken temporary vows in June. That this happened shortly after I'd taken another step in dedication to this vocation is another reason the incident was so shocking. I immediately went to the Mother Superior and told her that I needed to leave because I must be too selfish to live this kind of life. The Mother Superior said, "You will first need to get a letter of permission to leave from the Pope in Rome, but I will not let you leave for the reason you gave."

I left her office and returned a couple days later to tell her I did not know what other reason it could be. She again refused me. The third time, I told her I felt confident that this is what I should do, so she said she would start the paper work. In later years, when I looked back on her refusal, I realized how wise she was. She wanted to give me time to reconsider, and she did not want me to go through life thinking I was too selfish to become a nun.

Within a few days, one of the nuns drove me home. I immediately resumed the practice of going to Mass daily, and continued in fervent prayer for God to give me back the awesome **awareness** of **His presence**. For one solid month, I continued in this way without success, my heart breaking at times, pleading at times. Yes! One day in church--unlike all the other mornings—**there He was!** My heart filled with joy; the tears began to flow. My Jesus was there with me again! For about six weeks out of my life, I had the horrible experience to know what life would be like and feel like without Him. I pray it never happens again; I believe it won't.

The Father knew I would have stayed in the convent the rest of my life, and for some reason He wanted me to live a different life. I don't care where I am as long as I am with Him. His guidance and presence in our lives is a precious miracle.

We Saw His Face

CHAPTER 4

Mother and I were so excited! My brother called from
Florida where he was vacationing with his young family.
They were going to be there for three weeks and wanted
Mother and me to come join them. He offered to rent the
room next to theirs. Well, we could not resist. We left
early the next morning.

At four in the afternoon, it was high traffic time as we
drove through a city in Alabama. The road was four
lanes with cars bumper to bumper. The light turned red;
when I stopped, the car died. I tried and tried to start
it to no avail. We could not believe it! Of all places to
stall, we were first in line at the intersection.

I walked over a median and then a service road to a

gas station. It looked to sell only gasoline, but I walked over there anyway. The attendant said he could not help us and, at this time on a Saturday, the closest place with a wrecker and mechanic on duty was twenty miles away.

In a whole hour, only two different people stopped and looked at the engine to try to help us. We could not believe or understand that with so many people working their way around us, so few stopped to help. Mother and I stayed in the car, praying and singing praise and worship songs. We knew that our Lord would do something to help us. We had hotel reservations just three miles down the road but couldn't get there because we couldn't just leave our car and belongings in the middle of the street. Therefore, we just prayed and praised, expecting without doubt, that the Lord would rescue us.

A car pulled up behind us and stopped. I could see him in the side mirror when he got out of his car and walked toward us; he had a rag hanging out of his pocket. "Mother, he must be a mechanic," I said! As he approached the driver's side window and bent down to see if he could help, we both turned and looked to respond. However, I could not speak at first. My eyes could not believe; my heart, in an instant, melted. Finally, briefly, I did tell him what the problem was. He went in front to look under the hood. I turned and looked at Mother. Both of us had tears in our eyes. I said, "Did you see His face, His eyes?" "Yes, that was Jesus!" she answered. We saw a man with eyes so warm and so blue and hair to His shoulders with a neat beard. He looked exactly like the pictures you most often see of Jesus. But, when we looked into His eyes—that's when we knew.

After a few minutes, He said, "Start the car." It started right up! When He came around again, we gazed into His eyes as long as we could. We thanked Him and God, of course, and drove to our hotel. As you can imagine, we were floating on a cloud and couldn't stop talking about what we had experienced. It is an unmistakable, steadfast miracle truth that our God will be all we need whenever we have a need.

That face, those eyes my mother and I saw, never faded from our memory. We spoke of this from time to time over the next thirty years and each time we would find ourselves with tears of joy welling up inside. We had seen the **face of Jesus!** His eyes were so loving.

A Closer Walk

CHAPTER 5

On June 7, 1974, I had chosen to stay home instead of going wherever the rest of my family went—I can't remember. But then, the Lord arranged this as I was to see later. The phone rang. It was my oldest brother, who lives 165 miles away, calling to see what I was doing. He asked if it would be all right if he came to see me for an hour or two. That was strange. I said, "Are you here?" "No, but I could be in a few hours," he replied. "Ok, sure." I could not imagine what he wanted to talk to me about.

When he arrived, we visited a little and then he told me about his giving his life to Jesus, about salvation, and a special Spirit-inspired language he received.

Then he asked if I wanted to give my life to Christ. In my mind and heart, I thought I was as close to Jesus as I could get. After all, I had known, talked to, and been close to Him all my life. However, I told my brother, "Yes, because, if there is more of Him to have, then I want all I can get. I don't understand what you mean by more, but I certainly am not going to turn down anything concerning Jesus."

My brother prayed a simple salvation prayer as I knelt down, and I repeated the words after him. I felt nothing different at the time. He told me to begin reading a little of the Bible daily. After a while, he drove all the way back home. From time to time, he would call and ask if I was reading the Bible. I would say, "No, not yet." Finally, he said, "Just put the Bible I gave you by your bed and read at least one verse each night."

As I began doing this, I was drawn to read a little more. Then, as I would read, a certain verse would be absolutely magnetic or as if a strong light were shining on it, and it became so pertinent, so clear. It was as though Jesus were speaking directly to me through His words in the Bible.

In a couple of months, the opportunity came up for me to move in and share an apartment with my sister in the same town where my oldest and third oldest brothers lived. They were all going to a Spirit-filled non-denominational church, which I began attending also. It was wonderful! The worship was beautiful and the teaching was enabling me to grow stronger and closer to my sweet Jesus. Each week, I would go to services on Sunday morning, Sunday evening, and Wednesday evening. I saw people speaking in tongues. I wanted all there was that Jesus offered so one day, while praying at home in my apartment, I asked Jesus for a heavenly language. I just thought of Jesus and worshiped and loved Him mentally while giving Him my voice—"Ahhhhhhhhhhhhhhhhhhhhhhhhh." Low and behold, foreign sounding words began rolling off my tongue. *"Thank You, Jesus, for giving me a prayer language. Now, the Holy Spirit can intercede for me to the Father,"* I prayed. I could not believe it! I also, in time, by **faith**, learned of and practiced interpretation of this language, which is the inspired word of God.

Mother had told us about Jesus, and we could see her daily living her faith. All of us had a strong faith in God, but we were striving on our own to be good enough to get to Heaven. The Good News of salvation changed that as my brother shared his personal experience with each of us, and we gave our lives one by one to Jesus. Thereafter, to put **Jesus first** in our lives has been the goal of all seven brothers and sisters, and now, many of the twenty-four nieces and nephews.

My Lord and my God is so good! It is such a magnanimous miracle to have found that I could be even closer to my precious Jesus, that I could have more of Him and total assurance of Eternal Life with Him in Heaven.

A Moment of Revelation

CHAPTER 6

It was August 1974, and I was on the road en route
to Tennessee. What an exciting day! My sister had
lost her roommate to marriage so I was moving in with
her. I knew we would have a great time together. The
first thing I planned for Monday morning was to go
scouting for a salon in which I'd like to work; I am a
hair stylist. Hair salons were closed on Monday, but
I needed to check out the various areas of town first
anyway. I had a definite list of criteria to follow in picking out the right salon: near our apartment, successful,
with lots of windows, and a cheerful decor. My search
resulted in three shops of interest, which I checked out
the next day.

I had gotten up early, anxious to get started. All three of the shops I had considered failed the test. I then visited some of those I had formerly eliminated. Nothing was panning out; nothing was meeting my criteria. However, I had found the area of town where I'd really like to work. Salons are always looking for good stylists. I knew I was good in my profession and brought a portfolio of my work so I wasn't worried about getting hired, but I could not find the right salon.

Very frustrated, I went back to the apartment. My sister was at work; I was alone. I really felt at a loss as to what to do next and became disenchanted with the whole process. I fell across the bed and began to cry. *"I don't know where to go or what to do now, Lord,"* I prayed. *"None I have checked out are what I want."* I felt helpless and disillusioned. Somewhere in this tearful state, the Holy Spirit put a spotlight on the problem for me. Suddenly, I realized what I needed to do! It was time to use   **S.T.P.—Surrender, Trust, and Praise**.

The Lord had given this revelation knowledge to my oldest brother, through the inspiration of the Holy Spirit, and he had been teaching us about it. After weighing it for a few minutes, I decided to obey the Lord's gentle recommendation because I know how faithful He is.

*"Dear Jesus, I **surrender** to You. Wherever You want me to work is fine with me. I want to be where You want me to be," I prayed. "I don't care if it's a hole-in-the-wall place in any part of town that You choose. I only want to be where You want me. I **thank** You and **praise** You for wherever You put me to work because I **trust** You with my life."* Peace came over me immediately and stayed.

The next morning I got dressed and headed out the door but this time with peaceful **praises** on my lips and in my heart. I do not remember how I came to go to this particular shop, but I entered, talked to the owner, showed him the portfolio of my work and was hired that morning. The Holy Spirit had guided me there, of course.

Now, here is the miracle! This place was decorated in my favorite colors. It was unique in its design, which I loved. This shop was ten minutes from our apartment, and I found out later that it was the most popular, talked about salon in the city at the time. I had been in this profession for only two and one half years, so when my employer said that he wanted me to take part in an apprenticeship where he would train me in advanced European techniques while paying me a good salary, I was thrilled. This training proved to be invaluable to my career as a successful stylist for many years to come. I had opportunities to teach advanced classes on weekends in the salon, as well as do stage presentations and teaching at hair-seminars. This was not an ordinary salon; what it offered me was considerably above the norm.

I was amazed at what the Lord had done for me just because **I gave up my will to Him** to do with me, as

He knows best. He only wants us to **trust** Him without doubt, to lay down our will, **knowing** He is in **perfect control** with a **perfect plan** for us. What a miracle He is!

Psalm 16: 11

"You will show me the path of life;

In your presence is fullness of joy;

At your right hand are pleasures

forevermore."

Psalm 18: 30

"As for God, His way is perfect;

The word of the Lord is proven;

He is a shield to all who trust in Him."

Snow Skiing

CHAPTER 7

The weekend had come at last! Everything was in the car; we were ready to head for the mountains. My sister and I had never snow skied before, but now was the time. The trip was good; my sister is a lot of fun. After settling in our cabin in the woods, we headed for the ski lodge. The ski attendant informed us that earlier that morning they'd had a misty rain. He said, "After the rain, it turned colder so the ski surface is harder and somewhat bumpy in spots."

We rented all the gear and proceeded to carry it over to some chairs when two guys came over and offered to help. They put our ski shoes on for us and gave us a few tips. We were so relieved to have somebody with us who knew what they were doing.

Do not ask me why we were on the ski lift going up to the advanced ski slope instead of on the beginners. Maybe we checked in our common sense when we checked out the ski equipment. All I knew was that we were too high for my taste. Oh my goodness, here comes the place where we have to leap off the lift chair onto the skis we had never experienced before. I jumped—not too bad. Then my sister tried to jump, and her pants caught on something. One of the guys pulled her off, leaving a piece of her pants in the lift chair. This had not started off too well.

However, to our surprise, a ski instructor, employed by the lodge, helped us with the very basics. He said that to go slower, we should put our skis apart and swerve from side to side. To go faster, we should put our skis closer together and I figured--go straight.

We were both making our way slowly and carefully down the slope, falling from time to time. Thank goodness those guys were there to help us get back up! I guess we had been skiing about four hours when I decided I had the hang of this, and I wanted to go faster. The advanced slope had a sharp turn. If I missed it, I would end up running into dense forest. Also, after the turn, the slope took a decidedly steeper decline.

Cautiously, I began the descent, slowly to get the feel, then a little faster, but not too fast, because the devil turn was coming up. Oh, but I seem to be going faster than I thought I would. *"Oh my Lord, help me make this turn,"* I prayed! Somehow, I made the turn, but then I really started speeding. The snow was hard and rough. I was bouncing up totally off the surface and still going faster. At that point, I was scared to death! I thought, *If I could just sit down*, but then I figured I would hit, tumble, and probably break my neck, so I didn't know what to do. I just held my skis relatively close together, trying to keep my balance.

Desperately, I prayed, *"Dear Jesus, if you get me down*

to the bottom safely, I'll never do this again." Suddenly, before I even completed the prayer in my mind, **I felt impressions under each of my arms.** I was in total awe as I realized that an angel was supporting me under my arms. **I thought of this immediately as if I knew.** I floated down the rest of that steep slope as smoothly as if on a cloud. I remember what this felt like as if it happened yesterday. At the bottom of this mountain were bails of hay for people coming too fast to relatively softly **ram** into. However, I glided down slower and slower and, before I even got near the bails of hay, I just stopped.

It was the most wonderful feeling to know that I could call on Jesus for help and in a split second, help was there. I just couldn't get over it, even though I experienced it. I want everyone to know that the miracles derived from **calling on Jesus in faith** are real and true in **this** life in **this** world today.

A Woman Possessed

CHAPTER 8

It was a Wednesday church night in 1975. I was
tired and didn't really want to go. However, feeling
restless, I didn't want to stay home either. So I decided
to go and leave whenever I felt like it. The service was
inspiring as usual, and the music was great, but I was
just not with it. Feeling lethargic, I decided as soon as
the preacher finished speaking, I would head home to
bed. The singing started again. Everyone stood up, and
I slithered out. Walking to my car, I remember thinking
how wonderful the fresh air smelled and the breeze felt.
I was so glad to be out of there this night.

With key in hand, I reached for the door handle of
my car and heard, deep in my being, loud and clear,

but non verbally, "Go back inside." I did not want to, but it was so unmistakably clear that I had to. The weird part is, as I was going back in, everyone else was filing out. I could not imagine why I was going back in. I just wanted to go home to bed.

Inside a few people were milling about. Slipping into a seat in back, I prayed, *"Lord, what am I doing in here?"* The preacher was up on the platform talking to some people. Elders in the church were scattered around talking or praying for people. Shortly, I felt compelled to move forward. I got up and, as I approached the fifth or sixth row from the front, I noticed a woman lying on the floor in front of the platform where the preacher was. To the right, over a bit from the woman, was a cluster of four or five people talking. I sat down again just to observe. I knew that when individuals were prayed for that sometimes the Holy Spirit touched them in a special way, and this would leave them in a peaceful state for a few minutes. However, what bothered me about this woman was that she was coughing and squirming a little. **No one** was paying her any attention.

I knew what she needed; I wondered why no one was praying for her and commanding Satan to release her. Neither the preacher nor anyone else seemed to notice. I felt urged again to move up. When I reached the front row, my heart strongly went out to this woman. I began praying for her, reaching out my hand to her from my seat. My heart was beating faster now. I knew what I should do, but I could not understand why the Lord would have me lay hands on her when all these more qualified people were doing nothing. Could I be wrong about her need? I didn't know, but I had to act. The power of the Holy Spirit was so strong on me. I got up, gently knelt down beside her, and began praying inconspicuously. I rebuked Satan, commanded him to come out of her in the name of Jesus, and then just prayed in the Spirit. My eyes were closed, but they opened quickly when I heard her coughing hard and she then threw up a little. I prayed in the Spirit a little longer. Unbeknownst to me, her family came over. This was that group standing and talking over to the right of her. I will never forget, after a time when I opened my eyes, one of them looked at me and said, "Thank you."

I stood up, backed up a few feet and sat down again. You could have pushed me over with a feather as the Lord's peace came over me. I watched this woman; she was now very peaceful too. I walked back to my car in complete awe at what just happened. That night, I learned the miracle of the reality of God's word in the Holy Bible. **His word** and **His voice** in our hearts is as **real** and **true** today as when He spoke to the apostles on this earth.

The Wedding Dress

CHAPTER 9

While sharing an apartment with my sister, I became
acquainted with her best friend, Terry. We all had a lot
of fun together. One day a call came in from Terry asking both of us to be in her wedding, which was to be in
six months. I accepted and she wanted to know what
size dress to order. Hesitating, I said, "Can I call you
back tonight?"

After hanging up, I got on my knees and asked the
Lord what size I should order because I had been on
a diet and losing, but where would I be in six months?
Who knows? God knows! I prayed in the Spirit because
I knew He would tell me what I needed to know by
the time I had to call her back. During prayer, He told

me what size. I said to Jesus, *"I couldn't—it's too small!"* This was another time to use **S.T.P.—Surrender, Trust and Praise.** In the meantime, I just praised sweet Jesus because I trusted Him implicitly.

By evening, with confidence, I called her back and told her the size. She said, "Are you sure?" "Yes," I replied. This meant I had to lose forty pounds. I flat out ordered the dress in that size strictly by faith. I knew my Jesus honored faith. Even if I had heard Him wrong, I know that He honors our faith. I could do nothing but act on what I felt I heard Him say.

The Holy Spirit gave me strength and focus. Through His powerful guidance and my determination to do the Lord's will, the weight was coming off wonderfully. I was swimming fifty laps every day and eating healthy. I felt great!

The day came when the dress was delivered. I was so excited to try it on. The wedding was in two weeks. My roommate zipped it up for me as far as she could.

She said it **lacked two inches** to close! I was surprised since I had been very close to Jesus, spending a lot of time reading the Bible and in prayer, especially the last year and a half. I knew His voice in my heart. When the dress did not fit, I did not understand. I remember going into my bedroom, kneeling down, and telling Jesus, "I know You told me to order this size. Why doesn't it fit? What should I do?" I prayed in the Spirit praising and worshiping Him and thinking, *I trust Him no matter what. I completely surrender this to Him.*

The next day I went to work as usual and someone came in telling about some new product that helped people lose weight fast. It was liquid protein. She said, "You have to take it carefully so as not to hurt your health." I took it once a day at night and then only ate fruit. I continued swimming daily, ate light the other two meals, but wasn't hungry or suffering at all.

Believing what Jesus told me, "It will fit for the wedding," I never put that dress on again. I just thanked

Him for the protein and continued praising Him. The night of the rehearsal dinner, I just had to try it on. This was two weeks later. My roommate began zipping it up for me, but then I didn't feel anything, so I said, "Go on, I'm ready." "It's already zipped up," she said. I couldn't even feel it was the least bit snug, so I asked, "What do you mean?" "It is zipped all the way up!"

The miracle of Jesus' closeness to all our little personal daily problems and needs is very real. We must never think anything that is happening with us is unimportant to Him. His **love** is a miracle that touches every particle of our lives.

Follow Where He Leads

CHAPTER 10

After my sister got married, I had a new roommate for a year and a half before she decided to move back to her hometown, then I was alone for a while. I had lost interest in clubs and tried to meet Christian men. I had friends at church but not someone I wanted to date. During this time though, I really grew even closer to Jesus by listening to teachings from evangelists and ministers, reading my Bible daily, praying in the Spirit, and sometimes asking for an interpretation. My girlfriends and friends at work often asked me about Jesus. I loved telling them about Him.

One morning at work, my boss called me over to tell

me he wanted me to start working an extra day. I was already working twelve hours a day. Even so, this was a great place to work where I learned the latest techniques from Europe. My employer conducted classes and had us doing projects, experiments and research to improve our knowledge and skills into the night as late as 10:00 PM. This hair salon was the most popular one in the city at the time. It was a real blessing that the Lord had brought me here three years before, but I did not want to work an extra day. I told him so and he said, "Well, I want you to."

In the third year, I also had begun teaching advanced classes for hair stylists in our area and the surrounding cities. When there was a class, I worked Sunday and Monday also. Therefore, I looked at him and said, "I'll let you know tomorrow."

That night I got on my knees before my Jesus. I needed Him to tell me what **He** wanted me to do. However, **before I could hear Him** through the power of the Holy Spirit, I realized that **I had to give up my will—surrender.** I did not want to work an extra day, but I had to come to the place, and I did during prayer that night, where I could say and mean it, *"I will work an extra day, if it is Your will."* This is the way I left it before going to sleep.

In the morning, upon wakening, I began praying in the Spirit, *"Lord, Thy will be done. Just tell me what it is."* After awhile, I took a paper and pen and just began writing the words that came. The Lord said, "Go to work; tell your boss that you will be leaving in **two weeks.** Tell him you are moving twenty miles away to a little town and you want to work there. I will direct your path. I will show you where to live and work. First, look for the place of work. I will lead you."

I could not get over it! I read it again and again! I never even thought of doing anything like that, but I could not explain away the miracle that just had occurred. My Jesus flat out told me what He wanted me to do. I would do nothing else **but**.

Once I was at work, I felt a little leery of telling my boss this but only because of his predictable reaction. I was not the least bit afraid to upset my life by quitting my job and moving because I trusted Jesus so much that I knew He would not let me do anything that was not in His plan for my life, especially, when, truly and from my heart, I had given up My will to His last night. He knew I meant it.

My boss said, "You signed a contract." I had forgotten all about it. I did not say anything. The receptionist/bookkeeper was my best friend and she, without my knowing it, went back into the office and looked up my file. She came and told me, "Get this—your contract is up in **two weeks**." This was a clear confirmation to me from Jesus that I had heard Him correctly. I could hardly believe how He works when we let go and let Him guide our life. This was another opportunity to use S.T.P.—**Surrender, Trust and Praise**.

Once the decision was made, I had to scour the town for beauty salons. I got the phone book and proceeded to visit each one. You may remember that three years before, I had specific instructions in my prayer about the conditions of my work place, but I had learned since then. This time I just prayed, *"Thy will be done. Thank You, Jesus, for leading me where I can be a blessing for You."* At my present salon, I had a large solid client base. Nevertheless, even though I was moving twenty miles away, I knew that I had nothing to worry about because this was the Lord's plan, and in His plan, "...all things work together for good to those who love God, to those who are called according to His purpose." (Romans 8:28). I knew He had all the details worked out, if I just trusted Him completely.

I found just the right salon, of course, with nice people, and a nice atmosphere. In addition, I acquired an apartment in the same complex where my sister's best friend, and her husband lived. It was remarkable because all my customers, except four, followed me to this new location twenty miles away. All was well. I had a great job, a great place to live, friends, and I was growing closer to Jesus.

The miracle is that, if we **stay close** to Jesus, we can **know** He will **always** lead us and **never** let us get off **His path** for our lives, and **His path** is wonderful.

Roses From Heaven

CHAPTER 11

It was 1976. Independence was my middle name.
I loved the freedom that it brought: no ties, responsible
only for me, able to come and go as I pleased. Now
I realize this was a selfish attitude, but I did not see
that then. At twenty-eight years old, I said this prayer:
"Dear Jesus, please let me be married by the time I'm thirty,
but not before." Years later, I thought this was really
funny, but I was perfectly serious then. You see, I was
happy, but the loneliness was getting worse because the
club scene had become boring to me. The men were
fast talkers, but when it came to a conversation, I wondered if they had anything in their heads. One thing
was for sure; they could all lie. I'm sorry, but it's true. I

came to the point where I would actually come out and say, "Don't say things to me you don't mean. The only thing I want to know is, are you married? Please don't lie to me." Unbelievable, my little request was totally ignored! Thank goodness, I was living a Christian life because otherwise I would have suffered from the lies a lot more.

I did have dates, but after the second or third date, the guy would realize I was not giving in and would never call back. Some of these men I really clicked with; we laughed and had a good time. However, they must have considered me marriage material and they were not in the market, or they might have been married already, or they just wanted a sex partner. All I know is that I had had enough; I quit dating altogether. I was just plain tired of playing the game when they were not interested enough to get to know me as a person but only wanted a good time. No thanks. Besides, I also had too much respect for myself to be used like that.

For a year, I did not date enough to recall them. Now seriously approaching my thirtieth birthday, I truly was ever so lonely, not going out, so not meeting anybody new. I was in great shape spiritually and physically but not emotionally. I thought perhaps I needed to see a psychologist so I called the church I was attending and asked if they could refer me to a Christian psychologist; they did. I called, expecting to make an appointment, and the psychologist answered. He told me to write down all the highlights and lowlights during my whole life. I was to make two separate lists. Well, I began immediately writing memories of highlights from my childhood and continued up to the present. Then, I started a new sheet and found I had so few lowlights in my life that I should be more grateful. I saw what a blessed life I'd had and thanked Jesus for the wisdom of that doctor whom I never needed to see.

Months passed, and my discontent grew because I realized that my thirtieth birthday was getting closer and closer and that nothing was happening. It was only **eleven days** away. It was nine at night. I was working late alone. I locked the door behind my last customer of the day. Feeling especially low and lonely, I wondered what life would be if I had to go on like that. As I drove home through pouring rain, my mind was racing over the reason for my loneliness. *I would not be lonely if I just lived like the world lives.* I was crying so hard I had to pull over and stop. I remember pretending to pick up a gun at my side and bring it up to point at my head as if to kill myself, but then I thought that when they found me, they would say, "I don't understand why she did this. She was a pretty girl, very talented, had a good personality, and a wonderful family. It doesn't make any sense." Well, when I thought that, then I got mad at God for the first time in my life. I told Him, *"If you do not send me someone who I think is handsome to ask me out for dinner by my birthday, then I am going downtown in the city to Broadway and do whatever I want and it's going to be on Your head."* Please realize, I was desperately crying and at my wits end when I said this. I would never have followed through with my threat but I sure meant it at the time. So, that was it; I stopped crying. I felt I had reached a deal. The Lord had eleven days. On the rest of the drive home, peace came over me. Progress had been made.

The next morning I went to work as usual. Business is always good, thank goodness. I caught the phone mid-morning to schedule a new customer calling for a haircut. He didn't ask for anyone in particular so I put him down for me at 12:30 PM. I thought, *I'll just take a shorter lunch today.* He came in; I cut his hair. He was my age, and good looking with the prettiest ocean-blue eyes. As he paid me, he asked me out to lunch. I told him I couldn't go; that I had to work. The door closed behind him. I went back into my private styling room and immediately told God, *"That doesn't count; I said dinner."*

At about three that afternoon, a delivery came with

my name on it but no indication of who sent it. **It was a dozen long stem red roses.** I looked at those roses and knew exactly who they were from—Jesus. The Holy Spirit enlightened my mind immediately to see clearly that the guy had been sent by Jesus and that the roses were sent by Jesus to tell me that the Father had heard my cry, that I should relax and just trust Him with my life knowing He is aware of everything that is going on with me. Can you imagine receiving those beautiful expensive roses with your name on them and never hearing anything from the sender? Why would he send them? And remember, this happened the very next day after my ultimatum.

This left an indelible print on my faith in the Lord's miraculous presence in my everyday little life. In my spirit, I realized those roses were a miracle from Jesus saying, **"Trust Me; I am here; I have not forgotten you."**

Wholeness In Him

CHAPTER 12

Another year and a half passed. Involvement with the church I was attending kept me socially busy. I was trying to meet Christian men instead of just anyone. We singles had fun going out together after prayer meetings and on different group outings, but ultimately, I was very lonely. Everywhere I went I saw couples together and eventually I began to feel like a loner. Friends are great, but they do not take the place of a mate. I just was not meeting anyone in whom I was interested. From time to time, my oldest brother would say, "Maybe Jesus wants you to be His bride. Maybe He wants you to live just for Him without the distractions of marriage." Every time he mentioned that, I would get mad at him and storm away because I did not want to live my whole life on this earth alone. Poor Jesus, I must have hurt His feelings with my selfishness. After awhile, the Holy Spirit brought me to the place where I did **desire** to surrender my life to Jesus to the point of living **just for Him**, but I remember I could not say it to Him without crying. However, I did say it in prayer more than once.

Yet another birthday passed—thirty-two years old now. Some of the so-called Christian men I had dated over the last couple of years had also disappointed me by lacking credibility. I thought to myself, *For goodness sake, all I asked for was truthfulness! Why is it so hard for people to be genuine, up front, themselves? Oh well, whatever; I give up.*

A month later, one late night in January of 1979, after finishing all my clients and alone again, I sat in my styling chair thinking over my life: I had spent two years studying to become a Catholic nun; I had almost gotten married three different times, but changed my mind twice for the Lord's sake and once because I just wasn't sure. I thought about all the disappointing relationships I had experienced over the years and ultimately about what lay ahead of me. I was tired of it! I was ready to give in completely!

"Dear Jesus, I want to give You my future. I want to live the rest of my life for You. I want to be Yours alone for the rest of my life." Whoa, the devil didn't miss a beat! Immediately, as if whispering in my ear, "Yeh, but you might live a l-o-n-g life alone." But, just as quickly, Jesus came back and said, "How do you know? I might take you home to Heaven tomorrow." Satan did not say another word. However, Jesus did, **"When you wake up in the morning and open your eyes and realize you are alive, thank Me and praise Me for the gift of one more day to give Me praise, honor and glory and ask Me to teach you to think of others' needs and feelings before your own."** This happened

so clearly and precisely. It was amazing!

Therefore, for weeks that is exactly what I did. Oh, the freedom I felt! Each day I had only two things required of me and after obeying them, I felt free and lighthearted. I mean I would look at things differently. The sky, the trees—everything was more precious to me. It was not morbid at all. I simply looked at things as if life could be over at any time—today—tomorrow. I cherished what I saw around me in a profound and exhilarating way.

Work of course continued, along with church on Sunday morning and evening and a prayer group that met weekly. One week I walked into the prayer meeting as usual. People were milling about and talking before it started. I happened to walk in on the left side of the room and met up front one of the elders of the church I was attending. We said hello, spoke a little, and then he surprised me with, "Tell me what's happened to you." I said, "What do you mean?" He said,

"Tell me what's going on with you. What's happened to you?" I could not imagine to what he was referring. My mind began scanning the recent past when I said, "Nothing has happened. The only thing I can think of that's different is four weeks ago I gave my **future** to Jesus, and ever since I have had wonderful peace and joy with a new awareness of the beauty of God's creation." He said, "That's it! I knew something had happened to you. You're glowing with a light in your eyes."

Wow, I could not believe that he could actually see this. This experience taught me that **the more we give to God of ourselves, the more God can give of Himself to us.** I was **whole in Him—complete in Him.** If I lived the rest of my life on this earth alone, I would never be unfulfilled **as long as I lived for Him.** This miracle of God's wholeness will eliminate fear of loneliness because, when we truly completely give ourselves to Him, He fills us up with Himself.

Psalm 37 : 5, 7

"Commit your way to the Lord,

Trust in Him,

And He shall bring it to pass.

Rest in the Lord, and wait

Patiently for Him."

The Bridge

CHAPTER 13

It was nine o'clock at night when I started out in my car. My sister had called and said our mother was in the hospital. It was a three-hour drive, but I threw a few things together and headed home. The night was clear and the trip was going just fine. I was listening to praise and worship music and praying for my mother.

I was not driving recklessly, going only about three miles over the limit. I had crossed many overpasses on the interstate, but now on one, my car totally lost control. My steering wheel was not responding at all. The car began veering sharply to the left toward the concrete median guardrail. All I had time to say was, "**JESUS!**" Instantly—I mean instantly—my car just stopped going left and straightened right out. Now, I did not do it with the steering wheel because it would not respond. The car literally smoothly straightened out, and then, I felt the steering respond, after the car was straight. I just sat there going down the highway in utter amazement.

All I said was, "**JESUS!**" Wow! The **name of Jesus has miraculous power** for those who believe and call on Him. That's why we should speak to Jesus often during the day so that His name is in the forefront of our minds and on the tip of our tongues all the time.

The Father's Plan Unfolding

CHAPTER 14

It was March of 1979 and six weeks since giving my **future** to the Lord--dedicating the rest of my life to **live just for Him.** Recently, I had been thinking about how nice it would be to see if I could find an apartment in one of the old houses here in town. There were several big homes that had sections converted into rental apartments. In the past, I had always wanted everything to be new and modern, but I guess my taste was changing.

In the meantime, our church was having a retreat. I almost decided not to go, but then I told the devil to get away from me, in Jesus' name, and that I was going to forget about myself, just go on the retreat and love others. We all met at the church and rode buses out to the camp. It was fun. Upon arriving, we girls found the bunkhouse and proceeded to get settled. I was not in a hurry to go up to the building where everyone was gathering, so the others were finished putting things away before me. I told them I would meet them up there. I really took my time then and fixed my hair and lipstick, etc.

As I entered the main building, there was a couch on the right where the coats were being stacked. It was a cold crisp winter night. The room was very long and everybody was congregated way at the other end. I had to walk the whole length of the room before entering the crowd. Stepping into the group, I found myself smack-dab in front of a tall, distinguished-looking gentleman who peered down at me through his bifocals. We said, "Hello," and, after introductions, we exchanged a little small talk. He saw a diamond ring on my finger and asked me if I was married. I said, "No" and then I looked around for my girlfriends. I excused myself and went over to them. As soon as we finished our hellos, I found myself being pulled, as if by a magnet to look back at this man. *Why didn't I stay and talk to him longer?* I asked myself. I had always been attracted to older men. Then, my thoughts returned to enjoying my friends and I forgot about him.

One of the girls suggested we go into the other room and visit until the prayer meeting started. They passed through the doorway first. Just as I approached the door, this same man, whose name is Hans, appeared out of nowhere and said, "There is an empty seat next to the one with my Bible on it." I looked, said "OK," and proceeded to go over there to sit down. He did not follow me, but I wasn't even thinking of that anyway. After I sat down, I realized there were about two hundred empty seats except for the six my girlfriends occupied way over on the other side of that big room. Oh brother! Then I thought to myself, *Why are you sitting here in this seat all by yourself?* Yes, I answered myself, *because I want to.* At the time, I did not understand it myself.

The other people had begun coming in and filling the big room, but Hans did not sit down next to me until it started. At one point during the service, he leaned forward and, out of the corner of my eye, I saw his profile. I remember thinking, *not bad!*

The preaching was good and afterwards we all prayed together. Everyone held hands as we usually do during group prayer. The person on my left had taken my hand. Hans, now seated on my right, took my hand. As he did, something I can only describe as similar to electricity went through my hand, up my arm, and gradually all through my body. It startled me! *What **was** that?* I thought.

The prayer meeting was over and he left the room, so I went over to my friends. Food was being served in the other room, but we weren't hungry so we stayed and visited. After awhile, I noticed that Hans had come back into the room and was sitting by himself on a bench to the side. I remember thinking, *I'm not going to stay here with these girls; I'm going over there.* I am so glad that I did because we talked very easily, and I liked him. Then, we separated again.

Later, there was a short praise and worship service. Afterwards, Hans asked if I wanted to take a walk. That sounded great! It was cold, but the country air smelled and felt so good. As we walked, he told me about his life and we became better acquainted. The next day we were inseparable. At the time, I'm not sure if we realized there were still other people present--about two hundred. In fact, we were teased about this later.

That night, after the last meeting, we took a long walk again, talking and getting to know each other. It had been snowing big white flakes; it was so beautiful! We walked in it a long time. I began to wonder if the Lord was doing something. This all felt different. I surrendered to His will. That night, Hans told me he was going to marry me. However, I thought to myself, *I will not marry anyone, unless I **know** for sure it is God's will!* He walked me to the bunkhouse and gave me a gentle hug and a kiss on the cheek. *How refreshing--how sweet,* I thought. The next day was Sunday. We spent the rest of the retreat together, and then went our separate ways with plans to meet at our home church Sunday night. I told Hans I would pray about marriage and let him know my answer as soon as I knew. Monday morning, I told Jesus I did not want to marry anybody who was not in His plan. I had just recently given the Lord my future, and I was doing just fine alone. I did not want to get out of His will because I knew that would certainly bring unhappiness. I was not going to do anything unless the Lord made it perfectly clear to me. I decided that today I was going to stay before the Lord in prayer for as long as it took to get His answer about this. Therefore, at 10:00 AM, I began reading the Bible and, throughout the day, listened to Christian teaching tapes of different evangelist.

Around 3:45 PM, the tape I was listening to was the Evangelist Norval Hayes speaking from a large auditorium. He said, "If there is something you need an answer to right now, just stand up and worship the Lord. Raise your hands to Heaven and praise the Lord." Well, when I heard that, I thought, **This is it!** I jumped up, stood with my arms raised and pictured Jesus in my mind, while worshiping and praising Him in my heavenly prayer language. I do not know how long I worshiped. I do know that at some point **I was sure that I knew the will of the Father.** The thing is, **I was not thinking of what I needed, but only of Jesus.** It is still a miracle to me that at some point I stopped praying because I just **knew.** He obviously told me in my spirit through the power of the Holy Spirit.

The phone rang, Hans said, "Hello." I said, "Yes, I will marry you, because Jesus told me so." He said, "I already knew that." Then I shared with him the miraculous way the Holy Spirit revealed the Father's will to me.

On Wednesday we bought the rings and became engaged. I called my mother to ask if I could visit her the upcoming Saturday, and she told me that would be great because my four brothers were coming to have a meeting there. In the same occupation, independent of each other, they often had meetings to discuss business, but had not had a meeting at home for a couple of years. When I heard they were coming this precise weekend, I knew why. The Lord knew how important it would be to me for my family to meet this wonderful man before we got married.

Upon entering the house, there was much excitement at my bringing home a man without telling anyone. Hans met all my six brothers and sisters. We had dinner together and then I asked everyone to meet in the living room. We had a story to tell. My oldest brother, having my best interests at heart, was giving my fiancé the third degree at every chance he got. Knowing this, I walked alone outside into the night air before everyone gathered in the living room, and I put a "fleece" before the Lord. I said aloud, "Lord, after we tell the whole story, if my oldest brother does not agree, if he does not say it is all right, then I am not going to marry this man—period. I do not want anyone in my life or to do any thing that is not Your will."

The story took quite awhile to tell because I started with giving my future to the Lord six weeks before. To my amazement, when we were all finished, my oldest brother said, "Well, this certainly seems right." I was astonished because he was the first one to say something when we finished. The Lord had spoken again. He is so good. We need only ask and believe.

During that long weekend, we had planned our wedding, talked with the priest, set up the Mass, the reception, and had gotten our blood test. Even the courthouse dealings were taken care of. I do not understand how, except when it is the Lord's due season—His time—all flows like living water from Heaven. His angels go before us to prepare the way. We were married three weeks later in my hometown. We started our life together in one of those old homes about which the Lord had me already thinking. Twenty-seven years later, I am here to tell you, we have both grown even more in love with Jesus and each other.

The added bonus to this marriage made in Heaven—literally—is the seven-year-old precious gift I was given to care for and enjoy. Hans raised this little gentleman from eleven months to seven years by himself, and now the Lord had given me this privilege to share. *"Thank You, Father,"* I prayed.

This miracle, which unfolded before me, showed that we must give our Father all—all our desires, wishes, hopes and plans. We must give them up to Him. We must tell Him that we want only what He wants because what He has planned for us is always the best. We can trust Him with our lives.

Ride-em Cowgirl

CHAPTER 15

We had not been married long. One evening, while
getting ready for a prayer meeting, we were acting silly,
and my husband began chasing me. I ran through the
house and saw a chair in my path. It was a high-back
armchair. In a split second, I decided to go over it like
they do in the movies. You know—step on the seat
with one foot, then step onto the high back, and gradually push it over to the floor. Wow, it was working great
until…! There I was at the pinnacle of this maneuver,
about to push the back down with me in mid-air, when I
realized that this was his chair and I could break it. With
that second of hesitation, the chair and I came tumbling
down. My ankle was in great pain. This could have

been a great stunt if I had not second-guessed myself.

My husband of two weeks prayed for me immediately, put ice on it, and we thanked Jesus for healing.
We continued to get ready for the prayer meeting. At
the time, we were into cowboy boots and I thought they
might support my ankle better, so that's what I wore. At
the meeting, I had to stay seated after awhile. In fact, the
last half hour, I could not keep from crying; the pain was
excruciating. At the end, we would always stand in front
together, holding hands in prayer. This was a time for
personal requests. I stood on one foot the whole time. It
hurt so badly that I knew I would have to go to the hospital in any other situation.

My faith was strong, and I believed that if all these
people agreed in prayer and believed for my healing, we
would see a miracle. The Holy Spirit was moving power-
fully in my heart to take His words absolutely literally.
So, I had begun standing on that foot a little at a time,
rebuking Satan's lies and thanking Jesus for His **truth**.

When everyone else finished with prayer requests, full of praise and unwavering faith, I entered the big prayer circle and began walking back and forth. At first, I could only put down my toe for a second. However, with determination and assurance that my Jesus gave me His power over Satan and died on the cross for my sicknesses and diseases, (however stupidly inflicted) I became defiant against the horrific pain. *"Bring it on you liar,"* I told Satan silently. I knew that if I stood my ground in **praise** and **undoubting faith in Jesus' word**, the healing would have to be accomplished.

Sweating from the pain, I kept walking back and forth, praying in the Spirit and praising Jesus for my healing before the manifestation of it. I forced myself to gradually step down with more weight on that foot until after about fifteen or twenty minutes, I realized I was walking and skipping back and forth with no pain. I was, in fact, **healed!** Somewhere during my praising and worshiping, my ankle had stopped hurting completely. Earlier, I could not get my cowboy boot off. Now, it slipped right off.

All twenty or more of my prayer partners in that circle witnessed a true miracle from God, as promised to us by Jesus Christ, when we **actually take Him at His word.** Please know that Scripture is **real for today!** Some try to say that God's word cannot be taken literally. The next time we have a need of any kind, we should pick up our **Bible** and find His **promises** for our situation. Hold Him to it, believing without doubt. We can picture the Lord standing in front of us making the promises directly to us, because throughout Scripture He is speaking directly to us. **What do we have to lose—a miracle?**

Do not listen to naysayers! **See for yourself!** Jesus will honor our trust in Him every time. He will let us know in our spirit if we are to go to the doctor, and I would have too. However, this time I just knew that I knew Jesus was going to do a miracle that night for the edification of all of us there. Oh, what a wonder He is!

The Miracle Smile

CHAPTER 16

It was 1979 and we had been married for one month.
My husband had a seven-year-old son whom he raised
from eleven months old by himself. To encourage his
son's relationship with his birth mother, Hans let him
go to her home out west for the duration of our honey-
moon.

Oh, how I was looking forward to getting to know
this young man! He was due to fly home today, Tuesday, when the phone rang, "The flight was changed,"
his mother announced. "He will be coming Thursday."
Then, on Thursday morning, the phone rang, "I could
not get that Thursday flight; it will be Friday and I will
call you to let you know the flight schedule," she re-

ported. No call came, so we tried to call periodically on Friday to no avail. Saturday and Sunday were the same. By that time, Hans was very worried because this had happened before when his son had gone to visit his mother. "You go into a room and pray," I suggested. "I will go into another to pray." We did. It was Sunday evening.

In prayer, I asked Jesus to give my husband peace and to tell us both what, if anything, we should do. I prayed for his son's safety, then just worshiped and praised the Lord in my heavenly prayer language. After awhile, I became quiet before the Lord to be able to hear Him speak to my heart. I picked up a pen and paper and began to write down words that flowed from the Holy Spirit—not from my own constructed thoughts. He told us to get into the car, drive straight through the twelve hours, go to a school, approach his son's classroom, call him out, and take him home.

I said to the Lord, *"No way am I going to be a part*

of this unless You have told Hans, separate from me, the same thing." Well, after a bit, he came in to me and announced, "Something strange just happened." I said, "What?" "I was praying and I think I had a vision," he replied. Anxiously I said, "Tell me what you mean." "Well," he said, "I was at this school (he named it). I walked up the steps, went in, got my son, and brought him home." I said, "Look, read this." We were both astonished, but we knew that something was wrong and the Lord wanted us to go get Hans' son. We had no idea what to expect, but we knew that since it was the Lord's will, He would work out the details.

We drove all night. As my husband walked up the steps of the private school, I waited right outside the main entrance in what felt like the getaway car. It was a miracle from the Lord that Hans knew what school and where it was. I could not get over it. However, I was still praying that we do nothing out of the Father's will. Shortly, they both came walking out and got into the car. At the state line, Hans asked me to find a phone. He called the school to tell them that his son was all right so they would not worry; he informed them that he had sole custody. The principal told him that his son had been enrolled under a different last name.

"How did you get him?" the principal asked. "We have school security patrolling the halls, maintenance men on duty and teachers in every classroom. No one saw you come in or leave." Hans told me later, "I walked down one of the hallways, looked into the first classroom through the glass window in the door. All the students, along with the teacher, were kneeling on the floor with their heads down, praying. My son was the only one looking up right at the door. I motioned for him to come out. He got up, walked to the door and opened it. I closed it, and we walked down the hall and down the steps into the car." **What a miracle!**

About an hour from the school, this young man began crying because he did not get to say good-bye to his mother. I was driving; Hans' son was in the back seat. I was heartbroken for him, so I began praying, *"Lord, if he does not stop crying, smile, and be happy, I am turning this car around and taking him back, no matter what."* Before I could even get the last part of that prayer out in my mind, this young man interrupted me by pointing his arm straight out between us at some billboard and laughing at how funny it was. I stopped my prayer and turned to see his face. He was smiling and joking with his dad, and we never heard him cry for this again. I turned back to my driving, totally amazed at how fast and how clearly the Lord showed me that we were indeed in His will. Our Father will always direct us if we only **ask** and then **listen.** What a miracle to be able to communicate with our creator!

We had a wonderful trip home and settled into a normal good life together. Our newly-formed family life was full of fun and games, discipline and—most importantly—it was God centered. We prayed together and established a pattern of reading aloud a chapter out of the Bible each evening after dinner. I found that if I put the Bible on the table to remind us, we would all get up together and go into the living room to read right then; we would not scatter and get distracted. Often, we would discuss a verse and its meaning in real life, etc. This was a special time during which we bonded emotionally and spiritually. This practice was the cement in the harmony of our family because we turned to our common rock—**Jesus**—in all situations. We also used this time after Bible-reading and prayer for family meetings and fun games.

The miracle is the **power in the act of obedience** when we put our Lord and Savior **first!** His promises are **true!** When **love** and **prayer** are genuinely incorporated into the family unit, then no matter what imperfections we parents have, the Lord will overshadow in the hearts of our children.

My Will or His

CHAPTER 17

The church where my husband was to be a guest speaker was really filling up. The service was very good but I could not help thinking, on and off, about my mother who was visiting my brother, who lived nearby. We were going there after the service, and I couldn't wait. We are a very close family, and I love my mother very much. She is a lot of fun, and at the same time, highly respected.

After church, we rode in the pastor's car to the hotel where we had stayed the night before. Upon arriving, we said how much we had enjoyed his church and meeting him. Then he said, "You're coming over to the house for dinner. My wife didn't come to church this morning so she could prepare a good meal for you."

I **did not** want to go spend time with people I would probably never see again while my mother was a few miles away. I gave my husband an underground nudge but what could he say? "Of course, we would love to," he replied.

While they went in to check out of the hotel, I stayed outside. I was furious! I got out of the car and began walking in the parking lot, talking to God, "*I do not want to waste all afternoon with strangers. I want to be with my family. You know how much I love my mother and brother.*" All of a sudden, out of the clear blue, I heard a **voice** in my being as clear and loud as ever say, "If you give this time cheerfully to these people and genuinely love them, I will give your mother a long life." Tears welled up; never have I answered so fast. Aloud, I said, "OK, Lord, that's a deal! Thank You, Jesus! Thank You, Jesus! My mother is going to live a long life!"

Earlier, after my father's death, when I was eight years old and my youngest sister was two, I asked the Lord to let my mother live, at least, until my sister was sixteen. Somehow, I thought she would be able to handle my mother's death by that age. That prayer has already been answered.

On this Sunday, the Lord was asking me to give up my will for His and, even ahead of time, telling me of the huge reward awaiting me if I would let go and do things His way. A weight lifted off me; I was actually skipping a little back to the car. I was so excited because I **knew** I was going to do what Jesus asked and I **knew** He would do what He said. All of a sudden, I did not care if we stayed there two days. I **knew** and **trusted His voice!**

When Hans returned to the car, I was smiling—a totally different person than he had left a few minutes before. The lunch, the company, the afternoon was wonderful! God is so good!

The miracle: When we give Him our heart, mind, desires, will, and fears, He will give us abundantly above all we shall ask or think. His will is **perfect**; we must give Him ours. When we give Him time alone, we will **know** and **trust His voice.**

My Aching Back

CHAPTER 18

We were jumping rope. I was thirty-two years old and my stepson was seven. "Wow," I remarked, "This is easy," so I proceeded to jump faster on the concrete porch. But then I felt a sharp pain in my lower back. In tears at the chiropractor's office, I asked for help— "Please!" He knew what to do gradually to relieve my symptoms, but I had to go to bed for two solid weeks. Walking and sitting were too painful.

After two weeks, experiencing great improvement, I returned to work as a hair stylist. My ingenuity kicked in when I put a coke bottle case on its side to kneel on so I could shampoo my clients. Periodically, the pain would flare up. When it was bad, I would go out to my car, open the back door, lie on the seat, and pull my knees up to my chest a few times to relieve the pressure. Sometimes I would have an ice bag stuffed in my shirt into the waistband of my slacks to dull the pain while I worked. At that point, how it looked was not a concern.

During the next ten years, back pain would flare up more at times, but I would just go back to the chiropractor, do all I could, and it would become tolerable again. Often, in the early mornings, I would have to get up and soak in hot water to be sure that I could go to work that day. My son put my socks on for me more than once. Bless his heart. Ice bags were my buddy to numb the pain and relieve swelling.

This time was different. Relief was not coming, and I was tired of fooling with this back pain. As I read my Bible each day, the Scriptures that speak of Jesus ministering and praying for people always say, "...**all** that came to Him were healed," "...**everyone**," "...**any** kind of sickness (Matt. 4:23, 24), "...**all** those He touched" (Luke 4:40). I began to realize I did not have to live with this back pain the rest of my life. Plus, it seemed to be getting worse.

God's holy word states, "Anything you ask and believe, having no doubt, you shall have..." (Matt. 11:24). "If you have anything against anyone, go to them and reconcile..." (Mark 11:25, Matt. 6:15). "Sometimes evil spirits require prayer and fasting to call them out..." (Matt. 17:21). "Go to the elders of the church and have them anoint you with holy oil and pray for your healing..." (James 5:14). "Believe, expecting the evidence of things not seen..." (Heb. 11:1).

With my spirit fed from daily reading, reflecting on His word, praying in the Spirit, and still in so much pain, I decided I was going to follow those things Jesus outlined. The word of God had already strengthened my faith. First I made sure I held no grudge against anyone or I did not owe someone else reconciliation.

Then I fasted for two or three days eating only fruit. For me, this was a fast. I could not wait for Sunday morning to come to get my **promise** from Jesus, my Lord and my Savior who never lies, never fails us, whom we can **truly trust.**

Sunday morning, the pain was so bad that getting ready for church was just bearable. I stretched before getting behind the wheel and again upon arriving. The back seat worked pretty well for stretching, but I was hoping no one saw me. It had been about one hour and forty-five minutes into the service. At this point, I was fighting back the tears because the pain was so bad. My knuckles were sore from making a fist and pressing it into my lower back and against the back of the chair. Sitting was the worst. *"Dear Jesus, please let them announce that those who need healing should go out pretty soon,"* I pleaded.

Finally the announcement came! I could hardly walk though, after sitting so long. I made it to the prayer room where two elders and a little girl were. We were the only two who came for prayer that day. They were going to pray for her first and I, for a moment, thought, *I'm in so much pain; please pray for me first.* But, I didn't say that, of course. Anyway, they had begun to pray for the little girl, and I did too. Her illness was a respiratory problem. Then it hit me. I should stand in proxy for Hans who had just been told that he had emphysema. We were presently waiting on more tests to come back. So, while lifting up this precious little girl for Jesus' healing touch, I also lifted up my husband and realized that this was why I was in there with the little girl, as God's perfect plan goes.

It was my turn. After explaining my problem, they had me sit on a chair, take my shoes off, and stretch my legs straight out. Oh my goodness, as the elder supported my heels loosely in the palms of his hands, we all could see plainly that one of my legs was shorter than the other. In **faith**, we all began praying. The elders quoted Scriptures, rebuked Satan, anointed me

with holy oil, and commanded my leg to become normal **through the power of Jesus Christ**. I had my eyes
closed praying in the Spirit and praising Jesus for my
healing. When I opened my eyes, I will never forget
what I saw. The short leg was not as short and, as we
praised Him, it continued to come out until it was even
with the other one. They told me to stand and walk
around. As soon as I stood, I could tell my hips felt different. Whether I walked, or sat, or bent over, I felt no
more pain. **The sacrifice of Jesus Christ death on the
cross healed me!** It was amazing!

Shortly thereafter, I visited the chiropractor I had
been going to for the last ten years because I wanted
him to know what happened to me and, most importantly, I wanted to give Jesus the credit. It has been
fifteen years since my healing, and I have never had
to go to any doctor for my lower back. Furthermore,
my husband's test for emphysema came back negative,
even though the preliminary test came back positive,
and he has never had any evidence of it since his

healing. *"Oh, thank You, Jesus,"* I prayed!

The miracle is that God's word is **alive** for us **today.** Jesus personally heals our bodies just as He did when He walked on this earth. Let His word build our **faith** in His promises so we can expect miracles in our lives.

Isaiah 53: 5

"But He was wounded for our

transgressions,

He was bruised for our iniquities;

The chastisement for our peace

was upon Him,

And by His stripes we were healed."

Help for the Asking

CHAPTER 19

It was spring; we were heading to Florida, and all was well. Singing and playing games, my mother, stepfather, stepson, and his friend were all having a good time. We had rented a house near the beach.

After driving all day, we stopped at the grocery first thing and stocked up on goodies and the essentials. Then, we stopped at a little shop that sold stamps and cards. We were in a big parking lot with one lone car far at the other end. This probably used to be a busy shopping center. When we all got back into the car and started to pull out, we drove forward over an old foot high concrete parking barrier. We tried to push the car to force it over, but we were stuck. With all the groceries that needed refrigeration, there was only one thing to do—**pray!** We held hands and asked our Father in the name of Jesus to please let us know what to do or send someone to help us to the house. We were all tired and hungry. We were praising and thanking Him together standing next to the car.

I wondered whom we could call on a Saturday evening. As I was making my way back to the store, I looked up and saw a man walking toward me. He was a very broad man and over six foot three. He looked like a weight lifter. I was startled at first because he surprised me. I didn't see where he had come from. When a slight smile came over his face, I was relieved. "Are you having some trouble?" he asked.

"Yes, we drove over a big concrete thing and we're stuck," I said. Without the slightest hesitation, he walked over to the car, bent down, picked up the whole front of the car, and turned enough to put it down, away from the concrete barrier. "Praise You, Jesus!

Thank You, Jesus!" I blurted out. "Sir, thank you very much! You are so kind to help us! Thank you again!" He smiled and started back toward the store.

We were flabbergasted at what we had just witnessed! We were standing there somewhat frozen for a few seconds staring at the front of the car. Some of us turned to get another look at this man; "Where did he go?" We were parked a good distance from the entrance of the store, and no other car was in the lot except that one clear over at the other end. He could not possibly have gotten to the store that fast. I walked to the store to see if he was in there and noticed that the store had closed ten minutes before. The lights were out, and I could not see anyone. We all realized that the man who helped us must have been an angel! He seemed so kind and serene. He never really said more than, "Are you having some trouble?" We had just seen an angel sent from God to help us in our time of need as we called out in **faith** to our Father in Heaven.

The miracle is in **knowing** that our Father hears and knows all and that we can count on Him to get us out of jams and to safety. As **believers**, we are not out there on our own fending for ourselves. We have constant supervision and emergency help at our disposal. We need to just **ask** and **believe**. He will respond because He loves us so much.

Glimpses of Love

CHAPTER 20

For six weeks after giving my life to Jesus, I was totally in another place. Jesus let me see people through
His eyes and feel His kind of love—unselfish pure
love—for everyone I saw. I always wanted to care
about people like that. Wow, what a miraculous experience! I hope with God's grace, I can learn to love like
that all the time.

At a prayer meeting where my husband was giving
his testimony, I asked Jesus to let him refrain from calling on me. However, Hans asked me to come up front
with him to pray for people who came up for prayer.
That evening for some reason, I did not want to, but I
did anyway. As this woman approached me, I felt an

overwhelming **Godly love** for her—a compassion so strong. As I prayed for her with this powerful love in my heart, she fell out in the Spirit. When individuals are prayed for, sometimes the Holy Spirit touches them in a special way, and this leaves them in a peaceful state for a few minutes. I felt the Holy Spirit's power go into her and what a miracle that was!

When I hear someone's troubles and my heart breaks for them, or when I pray for people and tears begin to flow with earnest compassion, I know that this is **God's kind of love**. When I care more about someone else's feelings than my own, or listen to the Holy Spirit and hold back saying or doing something for another's sake, this is a miracle of **God's love** growing in me. When God's grace has enabled me to do something for someone, to fulfill a need with no strings attached, this is genuinely a miraculous act of **God's kind of love**.

We humans do not come by this **Godly love** naturally. So, when I find myself listening to the Holy Spirit speaking to my heart, guiding me in the ways of the Father and **actually acting accordingly—I know** it is a **miracle—a miracle of His divine promise to make me into His image.**

Philippians 1: 6

"...being confident of this very thing,

that He who has begun a good work

in you will complete it until the

day of Jesus Christ."

Fear Gripped Me

CHAPTER 21

Around the age of forty, I detected one of the symptoms of cervical cancer, so I called and made an appointment for a pap test. About a week later, they called me back in for a biopsy. After two weeks, the phone rang with the results. They had indeed found precancerous cells, and I was told to have a procedure done to see if the cells were invasive. All I heard was the word cancer.

Off the phone, my mind began to race, *Oh my God, oh my God!* Fear immediately gripped me! However, the Holy Spirit reminded me of God's word so, in my own words, I began speaking what I **knew** to be the **truth!** Alone in the house, I began speaking aloud to

Satan telling him who my Father is and telling him of the power I have in Jesus. "I am an heir to all that is my Father's and His power is in me because of His son Jesus. Satan, you cannot touch me! With the authority given me by my Father, I command you to give it up, devil of cancer! You cannot harm me in any way! You are as a puff of smoke, a fake, and I give you no ground in me, no place in me!

"I am heir to the King and all His promises! My Father is the creator of all and you have been defeated! I am whole and well because of what Jesus did for me 2000 years ago. You cannot hurt me, unless I give you permission and I **do not**! In Jesus' name, I command you, devil of cancer, to get out of my body **now!**" *"Father, Jesus, and Holy Spirit, thank You for what You did for me and all the promises You have made to me! I prayed.* ***I believe every single one of them and expect complete healing!"***

By the time, I finished praising and worshiping my

Lord and Savior and putting Satan in his place under my feet, I was **totally joyful and confident of complete healing.** But then, I knew that I must let go! I **surrendered** the method of healing He chose and I also **surrendered** completely to His plan for my future. I believed—without a shadow of a doubt—that I was healed, and in the same breath I gave myself completely to the Lord. **Thy will be done**—that was all I cared about or wanted. In the interim, I just praised and worshiped the Lord and did not worry at all. **(S.T.P.—Surrender, Trust, and Praise).**

One week after the procedure, I received a call saying, **"We did not find any precancerous cells."** I said, "What do you mean? I thought you did the procedure because of finding precancerous cells." She replied, "Yes, but when we went in and further dissected the tissue to test invasiveness, we found no evidence of **any** cancer related cells." After hanging up, I **praised** dear Jesus! *"Your promises have proven true again! I truly believe in Your holy words! Thank You, Jesus!"*

The **miracle power of believing**—having no doubt, holding Him to His word, and still letting go of our will is demonstrated throughout Scripture. The results of this kind of unwavering faith in God the Father, His son Jesus, and the Holy Spirit can be realized in our lives today, if we **believe**.

God Allows and Uses Suffering

CHAPTER 22

My sister called again. I drove home to Indiana the next day. Mother was suffering with a muscle spasm in her back between her shoulder blades. In the hospital, they did not know what to do to relieve the pain except give her morphine. Mother's doctor came in and told my sister and me, "I don't know what else to do. We have tried everything we know. We're only allowed to give her morphine for seven days and today is the last day."

"What do you mean?" I said. "What should we do next?" My sister and I were shocked when he answered, "I don't know." "We can't take her home!"

I stressed. "She will be in severe pain as soon as the morphine wears off! We cannot take her home suffering like that! What should we do?" The doctor actually shrugged his shoulders in silence. We could not believe our eyes!

My sister and I wiped the tears away and prayed for help. We asked one of the nurses where we could go. She mentioned the Mayo Clinic and Barnes Hospital in St. Louis. She said that these hospitals specialize in difficult cases. Immediately, we began making arrangements to take Mother to Barnes Hospital. We would need an ambulance quickly to get her there before the morphine wore off.

My husband called my customers and cancelled their appointments because I was not going to let my sister take care of Mother by herself. It was difficult following the ambulance. He drove about seventy-five miles per hour. We really had to stay alert for the two-hour drive.

The emergency room staff was expecting us so we

got in quickly. Over the next few hours, many doctors examined Mother, consulted with each other, and finally decided to try giving her tranquilizer shots right into the muscles. She received shots in her back and one in the stomach area. These did not work. She was suffering so much, quietly moaning, turning frequently. My sister and I were suffering too. It was hard to watch someone you love suffer so much. They tried electrodes, which administer thumping and pulsating motion to try to relax the muscle. Nothing was working; she was in such pain. Finally though, the nurse gave Mother something to make her sleep.

My sister and I had been praying through this whole ordeal, of course. It had gotten very late. We were exhausted and wondered where we could sleep that night, if at all. Then, the Lord so graciously provided a place reserved for a patient's family members from out of town. It was a true blessing. At least, we had three hours rest that first night.

The next morning, my sister and I were in Mother's room sitting at the foot of her bed—me to one side, her to the other by the window. We were being quiet to pray. I was reading a wonderful book that was feeding and strengthening my faith when my eyes fell on the words, "But this kind of demon will not leave unless you have prayed and **fasted**" (Matt. 17:21). So far, we had been rebuking Satan in Jesus' name and believed without doubt, but nothing was happening. When I read these words, it was as if a spotlight fell on the word **fasting**. I looked over at my sister and asked Jesus to tell her the same thing, to show me that this would make the difference. I just kept praising Him, sitting there with my eyes closed, and within a few moments, my sister said, "I feel the Lord is saying we should **fast**." Wow, we now knew the Lord was about to do something wonderful! We fasted and also we didn't talk, which for us was a bigger sacrifice. Instead, we spent the whole day late into the evening praising Jesus, worshiping Jesus, thanking Jesus for healing Mother and reminding

Satan of his brokenness in the light and power of Jesus.

Late that evening, we went back into Mother's room and found her squirming from pain. Again, we laid hands on her in prayer; but this time there was an overwhelming **spirit of joy** in what God was doing. Our faith, trust, and confidence were, through the Holy Spirit, at their peak. We prayed in our heavenly language after telling Satan that it was over. Satan truly has no power over us, unless we believe he does. At some point, we opened our eyes and saw Mother turn over on her stomach, put both arms up over her head, and start stretching as far as she could. Her legs were doing the same toward the foot of the bed. We knew that something miraculous was taking place in her body right then.

Full of awe, worship, and praise, and high on seeing the Holy Spirit's power at work, we slept well that night. The next morning, when we walked into our mother's room and saw her sitting up with her hair combed, that twinkle in her eyes, and her dimpled smile that takes your breath away, we both quietly screamed with joy. We could not talk fast enough to share what God did for her. She ate a big breakfast that morning for the first time in almost two weeks, and we took her home the next day. Her pain was extremely less severe and became less and less every day. **Oh, what joy we felt to see His power and truth!**

God uses all that He allows in our lives for a perfect purpose. Poor Mother suffered, but her girls grew in the knowledge of how He works, learned about the **sacrifice of praise** and saw His word come true before our very eyes. We were **drawn closer to the throne** through our precious Mother's suffering.

The miracle is that we can have His **peace** beyond understanding through trials, suffering and heartbreak, which enables us to actually **rejoice**, reveling in His love, care and promises. We can read Scripture to know what He promises us and **call on Him for everything in faith.**

Come With Me

CHAPTER 23

"Hi Mother, how are you doing, sweetie pie?" We talked and laughed for about an hour. This was Thursday night, September 17, 1998, years after the muscle spasm episode, and she was doing great. Then, late the following Sunday evening, the phone rang. It was my sister who lives in the same town with Mother. She said, "Mother had to take four nitroglycerin tablets Friday night but got no relief, so I took her to the emergency room. The doctor said she would be fine but he wanted to admit her to the hospital for more blood test. He thought Mother would be going home on Sunday. However, on Sunday he decided against it because he was considering other tests." I talked to Mother and she said not to rush home as I usually do because she would be home on Monday. She sounded like her peppy self, so I did not go Sunday night.

All night, in and out of sleep, I prayed for Mother and about whether I should go home and be with her and my sister. Even though, I usually go right away, this time I was not feeling that I was supposed to. This was causing me stress because I wanted to go and be of whatever help I could and to be close to them. Monday morning, I got on my knees and asked the Lord to tell me clearly what I should do. I didn't like it, but the answer was, "No." I called again only to discover that the doctor wanted to do a bone marrow test, which we had heard is very painful. My sister and I prayed on the phone that they would not do this test unless it was God's will and necessary. All day long, when I checked in with my mother and sister, they would tell me that the nurse kept coming in periodically saying that they would be in soon to get our Mother for the test. By

Monday evening, the test still had not been done or any other for that matter. It was the strangest thing, however, we knew that the Lord was in control and we kept praising Him. My will was really fighting against the will of the Father, but I would not disobey and head home. Although, I sure could not understand why He was saying, "No."

At about 7:00 PM, my sister called to ask my husband and me to pray for Mother because she had been so restless, even flailing about. While my husband led the prayer, I pictured the Father and Jesus on Their throne reaching down Their hands to my mother in the hospital bed. We asked that Their heavenly peace flow into Mother so she would rest peacefully. About ten minutes later, my sister called back and asked if we had prayed. "Yes, as soon as I hung up the phone." She said, "Mother is lying peacefully still for the first time in several hours." "*Praise God! Thank You, Jesus!*" I prayed. I still could not believe I wasn't there with them.

As the night wore on, I continued praising Him for her peace. My husband and I went to bed, but I couldn't sleep because I kept feeling like the Lord wanted me to get up and pray. I was tired so I didn't right away, but there was no denying it any longer. After midnight prayer on Tuesday, September 22, at 12:45 AM, this word came to me from the Lord God of Heaven and earth:

"Remembering your faithfulness to Me, I am going to tell you something about your mother. I have a **special place** prepared for her and you can be sure that she will be happy here with Me. I am not going to tell you the hour. I want you to focus on **where** she is going and the ultimate **joy** she will have here. You are not going to suffer long, if you focus on **where she is**.

"I am not going to let you or your sisters fall apart, if you **come to Me**. I am going to keep reminding you to focus on where she is—in the presence of the Father,

Son, and Holy Spirit. How can you not be happy for her? How can you not rejoice? If you really love her, you could only rejoice and praise Me for taking her home.

"Your Father in Heaven hears your prayers, loves you, and will not fail you. Show Him your faithfulness, and **trust** Him. Be at peace; you shall be with your mother again. I am preparing her, but it is not time yet. I will also prepare you and your faithful brothers and sisters. No one who spends time with Me daily is shocked about things that occur in life because I communicate My will as My children need to know. I am sending My angels to cover her so she will not feel anything. Do you believe Me? (*Yes, yes, Lord!*) Then relax and praise Me. I want your praise and worship. I and the Father are **one** and the Father and I are **one** with Our children who **trust Us**."

This word from the Lord was totally amazing, but I felt it strange that He was telling me about this stuff now. However, I thought, *It is nice to know that when it does come time in the future for my mother to go home to Heaven, I will get this out, reflect on it, and have peace.* Also, since the Lord said, "Be at peace; you shall be with your mother again," I did not allow myself to consider other interpretations. I thanked Jesus and went to bed to sleep.

It's still Tuesday, September 22, but early in the morning. At 5:15 AM, I woke up and immediately began praying for my mother that she would still be peaceful and not restless. There was no use trying any longer to go back to sleep because my mother was on my mind so strongly. I continued lifting her up to Jesus, praising Him for taking care of her, and praying in the Spirit. Suddenly though, I felt a strong desire to get up and kneel beside my bed to pray. I looked at the clock; it was 6:00 AM. I began praying in the Spirit and, in my mind, I was trying to picture Jesus and the Father reaching Their hands down to Mother to relax her the way I had the night before. However, I couldn't, because all I kept seeing were two figures in hooded robes standing, with their backs to me, beside my mother's bed in the hospital. I thought to myself, *That's not right.* I was still trying to picture the other, but couldn't. Finally, I realized that the Father and Son were standing by Mother's bed. I also saw big angels wings spread out around the head of the bed. I noticed that the two figures were standing slightly toward the foot end of the bed instead of up nearer the head. Later, I found out my sister was standing up by the head area. They were right beside my sister. When I told her later, she just loved that They were there with her. While preparing this miracle for others to read, I asked Jesus if I was right when I said that He and the Father were standing beside Mother's bed, because I didn't know if the Father would come down to earth like that. He said, "I was there; We were there. Leave it the way it is written."

The phone rang at 6:10 AM. I ran to answer it. It

was my sister. Without realizing anything ahead of time, I said, "Did Mother die?" She said, "Yes." I told her what I saw after she told me Mother died at 6:00 AM. I never once thought of Mother dying that morning. I didn't understand what I was seeing in my mind, but somewhere between the phone ringing and my sister saying hello, the Holy Spirit told me, and this made it so much easier on my sister. She didn't have to say it or be worried about my reaction. I was able to share the message I received the night before that made much more sense now and was a tremendous consolation to both of us.

At Mother's funeral, everyone was amazed at the **joy** and **peace** our whole family had. We knew we were experiencing **God's peace beyond understanding** because we were genuinely full of the **joy of the Lord.** It was another miracle!

Back home and facing work, I did not want to break down in front of my customers when they inquired

about my mother, so I asked the Lord Jesus to keep my
eyes on Him the way He told me. He gave me something to write down, and I looked at it every time my
mind started to fall into thinking about the sadness that
could be ahead. This is what He gave me: **"Rejoice
that your mother didn't suffer. Rejoice that she is
here with Me. Rejoice in the Lord always. Again,
I say, Rejoice."** The minute I felt the tears way down
there beginning to surface, I would just walk over to
my desk, and read those words a couple of times and
peace would flood my being. I had to rejoice because,
you see, Mother prayed—and we always prayed—that
the Lord would take her home without suffering a long
illness, or in pain, or that she would not live longer
than she could be independent. He had given us what
we prayed for—another miracle.

I couldn't help it; it always bothered me that I wasn't
there when my mother passed on to live with Jesus in
Heaven. We were always so close, and I went home

very often all those years—every four to six weeks for years and years—even after I was married. A couple of years later, I asked the Lord why He did not let me go to be with my mother and also, I asked Him why my sister had to handle those last days by herself. Then He opened my eyes and I have had peace about it ever since. You see, our youngest sister could not have been there in time because she lives farther away, so she would have been the only one of us girls missing from Mother's bedside. She would have carried that sadness with her the rest of her life because we girls were so close to our mother and to each other. Her Father in Heaven loved her too much for that, so I was to stay home too.

The miracle is that we need go **through nothing alone** in this world or be **unprepared for life** in any way, **if we stay close to our Father in Heaven by spending time alone in prayer and listening.** He loves us so much!

The Workshop

CHAPTER 24

My husband is a builder of big and small projects. He has a wonderful workshop and office adjacent to the house. He builds and refurbishes homes. In addition, he enjoys refinishing furniture, painting, and carving. He's very talented and creative. He loves his workshop so he fixed it up to his liking with four speakers strategically placed to give him a great sound effect.

One day I needed to speak to him about something. He was cutting long panels of wood sliding on a table saw. I never talk to him when he's using a saw because it's dangerous; he needs to concentrate, and the saw is very loud. I was just standing there watching when, instinctively, I reached over to help hold the panel of wood straight on the other side of the blade, which had no plastic cover over it. I just didn't see anything except what I was reaching for. My arm was completely extended and, in a split second, my whole arm swung out and then came flying back at me as if someone pushed it with force. I looked at Hans in utter amazement! In an instant, we realized what almost had happened. He turned off the saw and we just stood there, overtaken in silence. We both knew that I had come within two inches of cutting off my right hand.

When I could speak, I said, "An angel pushed my arm out of the way! There is no other explanation because I didn't even see the blade." For a stupidly negligent moment, I simply did not focus on the blade at all. Then, to my surprise, my arm flew across sideways and swung into me! Only after my arm went flying did I realize that there was any danger. An angel, my guardian angel, protected me from cutting my hand off!
"Oh, thank You, dear Jesus!" I prayed.

This occurred about six years ago. This is the first time I have spoken of it because before now, I would shutter at the mental picture of what nearly happened. It made me flinch inside so I pushed it out of my mind as fast as possible.

The Father said He would put His angels around and about us to protect us. He said we have favor in His eyes. Believe me; I know first hand that an angel protected me that day in a big way. This was another miracle of **supernatural intervention. "For He orders His angels to protect me wherever I go."** (Psalm 91:11) His words are true!

Psalm 91: 11

"For He shall give His angels

charge over you,

To keep you in all your ways."

Attention to Detail

CHAPTER 25

My husband, Hans, had vascular surgery today. During gall bladder surgery a couple of days ago, the surgeon found two aneurysms in my husband's stomach, each two inches in diameter. After further tests, the vascular surgeon found another aneurysm in the groin. He said that, if even one of those in the stomach had ruptured without our knowing, Hans would have died in minutes. All day I've been engaged in spiritual reading and prayer; I've had total peace. *"Thank You, Jesus!"* I prayed.

Hans went to surgery at 7:30 AM and came back at 3:00 PM. He was in and out of sleep, suffering with abdominal pain and pressure for two and a half hours.

They said it was air in the stomach from surgery. I was reading a book inspired by and teaching about the Holy Spirit. I had been in constant prayer and reading for two days and fasting. Reflecting on every sentence I read, and realizing the magnitude of its meaning, I had begun praying in the Spirit and worshiping God. I was sitting in a chair about six feet from my husband's bed. After awhile, I stretched out my arm toward him while praying in a whisper, although he wasn't wearing his hearing aids. He was sleeping and I did not want to wake him. After awhile, to my surprise, he said aloud, "Thank You, Jesus! Thank You, Jesus!" Just as suddenly, he was totally quiet again for a long time. I was stunned! I kept praying in the Spirit.

At some point, I felt drawn to place my hands on him so I got up and did that. I asked the Father, in Jesus' name, to let the **healing power of the Holy Spirit flow into Hans,** but as I asked, I could feel that happening already. I felt power—literally felt the indwelling of the Spirit. To describe this is hard, but I will try. While praying in the Spirit, my lungs were filling up with a slow, long, smooth, full-to-capacity breath—one deeper than any I could take on my own. If I were able to, it would feel as if I were going to burst. However, this was a light, almost radiant feeling that filled my whole body. It was as if air could pass through the body the way light passes through something transparent—yet the air was contained. Then it would begin to expel at a slow, smooth flow, but I was not doing it. The Holy Spirit was compelling my lungs to empty to what felt like the last drop of air in them. However, I did not have the horrible feeling of being the least bit out of air. This sensation did not feel bad at all. It felt like **power** going in and through me and coming out. I knew that at some point Hans was actually receiving the **healing power of the Holy Spirit** through my body. It seemed to go on for several minutes.

Hans had been sleeping all this time while I was still

praying in a faint whisper. I only slightly placed one hand on his stomach and one on his head, barely touching him because when he would wake up, he would have pain. Suddenly though, he began to say, "Thank You, Jesus! Oh Jesus, I have a miracle! Oh Jesus, I can't believe it!" He began speaking in tongues (his heavenly language). He said, "I've never felt like this, Jesus!" I continued in a silent whisper because I was having such a personal interchange experience in my prayer. I continued to praise the Father, Son, and Holy Spirit. Hans said again, "Oh Lord, Oh Jesus!" Then he said, "Amen, Jesus." During all of this, I wasn't sure if he was awake or sleeping because he never opened his eyes or said a word to me.

After a little while, he opened his eyes so I stopped praying, gave him something to drink, and sat down again. He kept saying, "Thank You, Jesus! I can't believe it; I am healed!" I was still worshiping and had begun praying in the Spirit again. I got up to pray for him some more when He said, "Honey, you should go home and get some rest." "I will, but not yet," I replied. "I feel like praying a little more." I laid hands on him again. Then he started saying, "Jesus, Oh Jesus, Thank You, Jesus!" The power of the Holy Spirit came on me again. Then, we were interrupted.

When the nurse left, I began to rub his feet while praying in the Spirit, praising, and worshiping the Father, Son, and Holy Spirit. I was led to pray for my husband to be healed of any bad memories of things that happened to him in his life. I felt the power flowing through me again—three times. All of a sudden, he said, "I don't know how I deserve You, Jesus. I'm not good enough. You don't know my soul." "God knows your soul," I said, "and He loves you and has healed you."

I prayed a little more, and then he said, "Come over here to this side." "OK, what do you want?" He said, "I want to get up to use the bathroom." He started to get up. "No, wait!" I said. He wanted me to put the bed rail down. Now, he had been told not to get up. He was to wait for permission from his surgeon. So far, he had only been up from recovery a few hours. He said, "I'm scared, but I have to get up." "Stop," I said, "ask the Lord if this is what you should do." He did and said again, "Put the bed rail down." "Wait," I said, "please let me pray and ask." So, I closed my eyes and asked if I should do it, and I sharply heard, "My Child, listen to your husband."

I had looked twice already for how to get the bed rail down while all this was going on, but the room was very dark and I always have trouble with them because it seems each bed operates differently. I was going to have to get the nurse to do it. In desperation, I said another fast silent prayer, putting a "fleece" before the Lord. "Lord, if I should let him get up, then show me how to get this rail down." The second I said that, my hand touched a lever down under the back of the rail, practically under the bed. I couldn't see it, but pushed. The

rail went down. I could not question the Lord anymore.
So, Hans put his hand around my neck and I put my
arms around his back and he sat up rather easily. As
soon as he had gotten three quarters of the way upright,
he began belching and belching and belching for about
ten times, at least. He thought he was getting up to
walk, which might have caused his wound to bleed or
tear, but it was just to belch. The Lord knew what would
get rid of the pain and pressure he was feeling. I was so
relieved and elated that Hans would be able to rest more
comfortably now.

The Lord's miracle guidance is always there in our
everyday lives to meet each and every need—if we **stay
close** to Him, **ask, believe,** and **expect** Him to answer
us. We need to spend time alone with Him each day to
come to know Him personally and intimately. Hans and
I praised the Lord, thanked Him, and asked Him to use
us to tell others about His loving companionship and
devotion.

James 1: 6-8

"But let him ask in faith, with no

doubting, for he who doubts is like

a wave of the sea driven and

tossed by the wind.

For let not that man suppose that he will

receive anything from the Lord;

he is a double-minded man,

unstable in all his ways."

The Gravel Truck

CHAPTER 26

Looking at the parking lot of my beauty salon, I realized it is time to order a load of gravel. I made the call, ordered twenty-four tons of three-quarter inch gravel, and was told they would be out in a couple of hours. Wow, I didn't expect it that fast! This is great! In the meantime, it began to sprinkle.

Time had passed since my husband's vascular surgery. However, since he was recovering from double hernia surgery, I told him not to lift a finger to help spread the gravel when it came. I would do it very carefully. Several years ago, I had watched him directing the spreading of gravel in my parking area. In addition, I once ordered it when he was in Europe. So

once again, I was planning how I want to ask the driver
to spread it. These big dump trucks that move dirt on a
construction site are huge. The tires are practically as
tall as I am. Even driving behind one of them in traffic
is scary.

Here he comes; I ran out to talk to the driver. He
was a nice man and very obliging. I gave him my plan,
asked him to lay the gravel like so, and he asked me to
direct him when to start and stop spreading in a given
area. It was going great. He had to turn around a
couple of times. He got in position again and watched
for my go signal. When we were down to the last area
where I needed him to spread the remaining gravel, I
asked him to count to five to drop some extra gravel
in this one low spot and then to drive on to spread the
remainder. He said, "There isn't much left. I'll drop
the rest in the low spot." Having had experience at
pushing gravel around, I said, "Are you sure there isn't
much, because I just want a little extra here—not a

lot?" He checked to see how much there was and then said, "Yes, I'm sure."

He climbed up into the truck, opened the back and it came pouring, and pouring, and pouring out. All the while, I was motioning and yelling, "Move forward; move forward!" He did not see or hear me. I could not believe my eyes! In the middle of my beautiful newly graveled parking lot was a three-foot pile of gravel the width of the truck. I already had a shovel and hard rake out there because I knew there would always be a little I had to push around. When he got out of the truck, I had them in my hand and held one out to him, "Looks like we have some shoveling to do." I did not give him an option because I could not move all this gravel by myself. Moreover, he should have known better than to have dropped all of it in one spot.

After pulling his truck forward out of the way, we began the backbreaking undertaking. I prayed for both of us that we would not hurt our backs. From past experience, I learned that with this kind of work, if I bend my knees, using my legs and my arms instead of my back to push or pull the gravel with the rake, I won't hurt myself. He was shoveling which, of course, involves lifting.

It was raining a fine mist as we worked. Somehow, we got that hump spread out and down about two thirds. "Can you drive over it a few times with your heavy truck?" I asked. "Maybe it will press it down enough. I don't care if it's a little higher because it will sink in time." He said, "OK" and proceeded to do so.

Boy, that did the trick! I got my checkbook to pay him. I felt sorry for him because he was really breathing hard from moving all that water-soaked gravel. I told him how much I appreciated him and thanked him for staying and helping me. He climbed up into the truck again, and **I watched as he moved forward and out into the street.** When I was confident he was leaving, I turned around to continue pushing and moving gravel to level it out even more. I was getting really tired and seriously focusing on protecting my back by holding onto the rake handle three quarters of the way down to the ground. With my knees bent even more—practically squatting—I thought, I'll do just a little more. The handle of my rake was sticking out behind me because of the way I was holding it.

All of a sudden, the rake was knocked out of my hands from behind and I lunged forward to the ground. While on my hands and knees, I turned my head to look over my shoulder at what knocked the rake out of my hand. I saw a big truck tire coming right at me. I had no time to think! Suddenly, my body was involuntarily tossed around—similar to what it felt like once when I was swiveled and tumbled beyond my control while being caught in too big a wave. Both my legs flew out from under me up into the air; I landed on my back. Then, swung with momentum to the right, my legs seemed to pull my body over, and then I rolled completely head over heel and landed on my feet. Those big tires rolled past two feet in from of me. I just stood there in awe of what had just happened because **I knew that I did not do it.**

The driver apparently saw me standing close to the side of the truck from his passenger side mirror because he came running out to ask, "Are you OK?" I said, "Yes, but I was just saved from being crushed by that back tire! **My guardian angel saved me!**" I should have been devastated, but instead, I could not wait to tell him about the miracle that just saved my life. As I picked the gravel out of my hands, I asked him, "What were you doing?" He said, "When I looked out my driver side mirror, as I was pulling out onto the street, I saw the hump of gravel and thought I would back over it one more time for you." After he left, I remembered there should have been a beeping device on that truck when it backs up. Thank God, he was driving very slowly. I had been wearing a warm scarf, and I was leaning low to the ground moving the gravel. I did not hear that truck at all.

It has been a year. I have not been able to even think about this near death experience until now though, because it made me cringe. I can still vividly remember the sharp gravel against the back of my neck and head as I flipped over onto my feet. I **knew**, could never prove, but **knew what happened to me.**

Well, I was horrified at what **almost** happened and, at the same time, elated at what **did** happen. I was maneuvered free from this dangerous predicament **miraculously.** My heart was beating a mile a minute, so I went up and sat on the porch in sort of a state of shock, thinking that I would never tell my husband of this incident because I did not want him to have a mental picture of what could have happened. I still have not told him at the time of this writing.

We are not at the mercy of this world. The Father **promises** miracle power in our life. We can truly

believe His word and **expect** Divine intervention.

What a miracle!

Psalm 103: 20

"Bless the Lord, you His angels,

Who excell in strength,

Who do His word."

Psalm 91: 12

"In their hands they shall

bear you up,

Lest you dash your foot

against a stone."

I Will Prepare You

CHAPTER 27

(8:30 AM Prayer Time—the Holy Spirit is speaking to my heart).

"My comfort I give you. In My presence, you will find such peaceful existence. Each and every—good or bad—situation will be conspicuously **from Me** or **allowed by Me**. Therefore, you will realize there is no need for alarm. Rejoice in each situation knowing I am in control. Just ask, what do You want me to learn from this, Lord? Rejoice, knowing I will lead you triumphantly through all that I ask of you. Just be at peace knowing I am handling it. Sit back, praising and worshiping Me in expectation of how I will work the Father's perfect will, which is always for your good. Alleluia!

"Have the presence of mind to see the situations that arise in your life from this true point of view and nothing will ruffle you. You know it is **from Me** or **allowed by Me**; therefore, I will handle it to the good for those who **trust Me**." *"Thank You, Jesus, for telling me how to maintain joy in my life,"* I prayed.

(9:45 PM that evening)

My husband had to take me to the emergency room with severe abdominal pain. I was admitted to the hospital after x-rays and blood test. The next day I had an Ultra Sound, CT scan and two more blood tests before hearing exactly what my problem was. The next afternoon, I had my gall bladder removed, which was diseased and full of stones. Come to find out, the doctor was concerned it might have affected my pancreas, which would have been more serious. Also, because of swelling for several months, he checked for cancer.

The reason I mention all of this is that, after I returned home and reread the Lord's words for the day of my attack, I realized He was clearly preparing me for what was coming. The miracle is that when we stay close to Him, spend time with Him, remain alert to His voice, we will never be shocked or unprepared. In the hospital, when I began to lose heart because of having to wait for all the tests and results, I just prayed, *"Jesus, give me Your peace; give me Your strength"* and He did. In His word, He promised He would. *"Thank You, Lord, for taking such good care of me; You always do."* The surgery and recovery were very easy.

Psalm 138: 7-8

"Though I walk in the midst of trouble,

you will revive me,

You will stretch out Your hand...

And Your right hand will save me.

The Lord will perfect that which

concerns me,

Your mercy, O Lord, endures forever."

Testimony of His Work

CHAPTER 28

It was the last day in the hospital after gall bladder surgery. My hip socket had become inflamed and was very painful. Maybe the position they had me in during surgery or the horribly soft mattress I laid on for three days caused it.

Back at home, my hip was not getting better at all. I was starting to get teary-eyed worrying about being able to take care of my customers who rely on me to do their hair. But then I thought, *No, all I have to do is ask Jesus to let me be healed by the time I need to work and I will be.* So I did that and surrendered the situation to the Lord. Then I was just thanking and praising Him, believing ahead of time, without doubt, in His perfect plan. **(S.T.P.—Surrender, Trust, and Praise)**.

We had arranged to go to an out-of-town wedding so I had marked off extra days. *"Father in Heaven, thank You for letting this happen at a time when I have to move only two days of customers,"* I prayed. *"Dear Jesus, please let me know how to reschedule them for their good and mine."* Later again I prayed, *"Dear Lord, You answered my prayer, as usual. The rescheduling went very smoothly. Thank You, dear Jesus! Lord, what do You want me to learn from this that You allowed?"* He answered, "I want you to learn compassion and tenderness for the suffering of others who do not know Me."

Approximately 7:00 PM that evening, I had just finished typing what the Lord miraculously compiled, taking excerpts from several months of messages He had given me during daily prayer time. This was for two people who were not Born-Again Christians. One believed in God and the other was not sure. The former had just found out he had a bladder full of cancer, and also cancer in his lungs and in his brain the size of an egg. I was in total awe and found myself in tears while typing, watching how Jesus was using me to do this wonderful work, through the **power of the Holy Spirit**, to send these two people His messages of **hope, salvation** and **peace**. I did not figure it out myself—what to pick, how it would fit together or anything.

As I started to type, I asked Jesus to let me know what to put when and where. Each time I turned to the next section He had me to mark for them earlier, I could not believe how each piece fit perfectly together with the next as if it were all written at one time. This was truly a miracle I will never forget—to have experienced that smooth, peaceful, easy guidance to accomplish something I normally would have had to spend hours deciphering and trying to fit together. He had chosen them so that, from beginning to end, the message to these two people was a loving and gentle **call** to **know** Him personally and lead them to **salvation**. All I did was type the messages and sent them for Him.

Before I started, I was in a lot of pain; I could hardly walk. When the Lord put it on my heart to type the messages He had picked out, the first thing I thought of was that I would not be able to sit that long. Then the Holy Spirit spoke to my heart and I responded, *"Lord, I bet if I obey and do what You ask, You will heal my hip because You said that if we are in Your will, we can ask anything, having no doubt, and we shall have it. Therefore, I will type these messages and I thank You and trust You to heal my hip. I **know** it's done."* I typed for four hours and had no pain! The Lord completely healed my hip by the time I had to go to work two days later! I knew the Lord would honor my obedience. He is so amazing!

There are so many miracles here. All we have to do is stay in tune with our precious Lord. We must **listen** for His voice in our hearts and **don't ignore it** because the blessings are so beautiful and truly miraculous.

Too Sharp for Me

CHAPTER 29

(9:00 AM Prayer Time—the Holy Spirit is speaking
to my heart).

"History has shown how present to man that I am in
everyday life and situations. I wait for My children to
call on Me. I love to be there for you, solve your problems and meet your needs. If only man could get the
real magnitude of this truth. I want to cover you in all
things.

"My child, you are going to see My miracle power
again today. Do you believe Me?" "Yes, Lord," I responded. "Count it all learning, My child, but do not
find yourself having to learn the same things over and
over. Then your service is delayed and less effective.

I cannot call on you to do things that take boldness if you are questioning My voice all the time. Remember: **rather act in error than not to act at all.**"

About 4:00 PM the same day, I cut my finger with a new big knife my husband bought us. He was gone at the time. The cut was deep! I immediately saw that I needed to go to the emergency room, so I held it together tightly, rebuked Satan, and prayed in the Spirit, asking for healing.

Since I take an aspirin each day, a cut takes awhile to stop bleeding; this time was different. After a couple of minutes, I noticed that the blood stopped dripping into the sink. I was holding it tightly just until I could compose myself and get something around it to get to the hospital, but it stopped bleeding long enough for me to let go so I could see it again. It did not pull apart again at all! The skin looked fused together where that deep cut was just minutes before. I knew I had just witnessed a miracle! I was elated! After binding it with thick gauze and big bandages wrapped tightly, I prayed it would not start bleeding again. I kept it dry by using a plastic glove and in a couple of days, I could hardly see where the cut had been. Oh, what a wonder our Lord is! I was so relieved not to have to go to all the trouble of going to the emergency room and waste all that time.

At some point later that week, I realized what the Lord had said to me: **"You are going to see My miracle power again today. Do you believe Me?"** Wow! How can we ever doubt when we see such blatant proof of Jesus' closeness to our lives? The real miracle is that **His promises** are true and He expects us to count on them in everyday situations. Jesus wants us to rely on Him for **all** of life.

Matthew 9: 28-29

"...Do you believe that I am

able to do this? ...According to

your faith let it be to you."

The Miracles Add Up

CHAPTER 30

What a surprise! My sister, brother-in law, and their two daughters drove three hours to surprise my husband on his birthday in May with a brand new computer and printer. Oh, what a Blessing! They set it up, showed us the basics, ate pizza, and drove three hours back home, having to go to work the next day. My husband is retired and speaks or at least understands several languages, so with computer access to the internet, he can read newspapers from foreign countries. What a thoughtful sweet gift!

Up to this point, my attitude toward computers was: I don't need one; if I had one, it would just be a toy; I don't have time to waste fooling around on one because I can't get everything done I need to do as it is. However, I wanted to help my husband understand how to use it. Therefore, I began reading the instruction book, diligently underlining important information and trying to apply it so I could show him. He is much smarter than I am, but not the studious type. He would rather try to figure it out himself, but I was afraid he would get frustrated and give up in this endeavor.

My sister and her family also bought a Microsoft Word program that offered a seven-day span of time in which I could choose from a long list of tutorials. Because they paid for this, I was determined to get the most out of it. In addition to working in my business, I found twenty-seven hours to spend one week on classes and took extensive notes so I could refer to the material when I really knew better what they were talking about. There must have been enough material there for three weeks. I got the most I could get out of those seven days. At times, I would pause in brain overload and ask myself, *Why am I doing this? I don't need to know this stuff.* Nevertheless, somehow, I was driven.

I began playing around with Easy Designer, which enabled me to design amateur Web pages very simply, formatting text using templates and sprucing them up with pictures. I kept studying the books and calling the helpline to learn more. Many times I was so exhausted and frustrated, but to my dismay, I did not want to give up. I just had to try to learn whatever I came upon that I did not understand. Little did I know that the Holy Spirit was urging me on.

At some point, it came to me. With a Web site, I could document messages the Lord had been giving me during prayer time since 1997, but I had no idea how to go about it. Instead of typing these messages with a normal typewriter, as I had been doing for the last year or so, I started typing and saving them to Microsoft Word.

It was around Christmas, and the Web site idea was

not going away. I mentioned to my son that I thought the Lord wanted me to have a Web site. He right away said, "Call R. S.; that's what he does for a living." R. S. went to school with my son. He is a Christian and lives three doors down the street. I felt inadequate and insecure talking to anyone about the computer much less about a Web site. I had no idea what it really involved. I thought I would rather deal with a stranger. Then, if I looked stupid, at least that person wouldn't know me. The next morning, I looked in the phone book for Web site designers. I found three in my area. It was 10:00 AM Monday morning, when I dialed one number and no one answered. What a relief! However, since this is a business, I figured I must have dialed wrong. I dialed again—no answer.

Dialing the second number, I took a deep breath—no answer. *What is going on?* I thought. I dialed again— no answer. *Oh brother! All right, here goes the last number.* Ringing—answered. I explained that I needed information on having a Web site designed, what all was involved, and the cost. He said, "Sure I'll connect you with the president of the company." I said, "Is that who I would be dealing with?" He said, "Yes." I freaked out and hung up; that was too intimidating. I knew too little to know if I would be railroaded or not. I felt too vulnerable. I had taken all those classes, but there was too much information in too short a time to have all of it understood without practical application. I sat there realizing what the Lord had just done. I heard in my spirit, "Now, will you call R. S.?" There and then, I decided to call. We made an appointment for him to come to the house in a few days.

When we step out in faith, the Holy Spirit moves. Between the time that I made that phone call to R. S. and our appointment, I was told in my prayer time to prepare a possible home page and introduction, which later became my personal note on the Web site, and a mock up of my thoughts on what the message pages would look like and entail. For each page of the Web site, the Holy Spirit led me to have a key phrase, a pretty picture, the date, and the message given on that date.

It was embarrassing to show R.S. this presentation because I didn't know if it would be silly, but I was just following what the Holy Spirit had guided me to do. To my surprise, after my presentation, he said, "This is great! Most people don't have any idea what they want." *Oh my, what a relief!* I thought. The Lord had shown me in my spirit what He wanted.

Over time, we fine-tuned the Web site and got it just where the Lord wanted it. However, about three weeks before I actually started entering messages, the Lord put something else on my heart, and I did not like it at all!

During prayer time one morning, He told me to buy a laptop computer. Well, there was **no way!** I don't know how this came up or why, but I unequivocally did

not need another computer. There are only the two of us, and I do not believe in waste or having more of something than one needs. As soon as I told my husband, he said, "Yes, that is what you need." I got mad at him for saying that. There was no way I was getting a second computer in this house; that would be utterly preposterous!

I put that idea out of my mind immediately, but unfortunately, it would not stay out. All I remember is torment and unrest. For two weeks, I drove my husband crazy because I kept saying, "I am not getting another computer!" And he would say, "I know; I heard you." I was miserable because I knew the Lord had told me to buy a laptop, but **I did not want it!** Naturally, in this state of disobedience and willfulness, I was wearing out.

Finally, after two weeks, I came into the living room and made an announcement. "I cannot take it anymore! Tomorrow, I am going to buy a laptop computer.

Will you go with me? **But**, when I get home, if I do not have peace, it's going right back." We did go, and I did get it. At home, I plugged it in, got it going and familiarized myself with it for a couple of hours, getting things set up, etc. When I took a break, I went to my husband and said, "I **already know why** the Lord had me get this. With the laptop, the position of my neck, shoulders, and wrists is totally relaxing. My neck isn't cricked up, and my wrists rest in a natural position while I type." In contrast, after many hours spent on my husband's desktop typing messages, I was already having neck and wrist pain. I had never realized that a laptop would be so accommodating; **my Jesus knew**.

"Lord, you are totally unbelievable!" I prayed. *"When I look back on the sixteen-hour days of typing Your messages on Your Web site, I realize how thoughtful You are, dear Jesus. We were to take a long trip that winter with three weeks off, but You knew we would not be taking the trip after all. Instead, You gave me three weeks to focus*

exclusively on getting started putting Your messages on Your Web site, **www.hiscompanionship.com.** *Thank You, dear Jesus!"*

My sweet husband fixed our meals, cleaned, and kept up with the laundry. He sacrificed during those weeks because of my time spent in service to the Lord, but he knows how important obedience to a call from the Lord is.

The Lord gave me extraordinary stamina during that period. I would get up at four or five in the morning and steadily work on His Web site until nine at night. Even while I was entering one message after another, for a moment I'd wonder how I was keeping on. As I stopped to ponder this, I knew I was being urged on supernaturally. There was no way I could have endured that long—day after day. By nine at night, my eyes were burning, but I felt great. His power was pouring into me. Because of my obedience, the Holy Spirit provided the knowledge and strength for me to persevere.

Each day felt like another miracle and the messages were feeding me, filling me up with His **love**.

It took me one and a half years to enter seven years of messages. Satan often tried to discourage me by putting his thoughts in my mind as I typed. "You're wasting your time; you're going to make a fool of yourself when people you know read them. What are people going to think about you when they realize that you're saying that God talks to you?" He went on and on. I had to stop every once in awhile, look up to the picture of Jesus above my desk, and tell Satan to "Get Lost!" in Jesus' name because, no matter what, I wanted to obey my Lord and Savior. He is all **loving** and all **knowing** and I **trust** Him **above all else**. Peace would replace torment again and again.

Any time I had trouble with a complex sentence that I just wasn't sure about, I'd finally look up to Him and ask, "Jesus, what do you want to say here?" Amazingly, every single time, by the time I looked down from His picture on the wall to the computer screen and reread the sentence, I knew how to fix it easily. I just shook my head in awe, wishing that everyone **knew** how **close** and **accessible** He is. Tears would come to my eyes because I knew something priceless I could never prove to anyone. Each of us has to find it for ourselves by **trusting Him** and **stepping out in faith**.

The miracle is that if we **listen** and **obey**, we get to accomplish things beyond ourselves through a power greater than ourselves and witness the Father's perfect plan in motion.

James 1: 5

"If any of you lacks wisdom, let him

ask of God, who gives to all liberally

and without reproach, and it will

be given to him."

Luke 12: 43, 47

"Blessed is that servant whom his master

will find so doing when He comes.

And that servant who knew his master's

will, and did not prepare himself or do

according to His will, shall be beaten

with many stripes."

Stop! It's His Plan

CHAPTER 31

As I typed the Lord's words, I knew they were important. He planted the seed of an idea to get this message out to people. I made a copy of it and laid it over
the fireplace. My husband saw it later and said, "This
is really powerful!" "I know," I said, still feeling surprised by its wording and relevance.

By the next day, I knew I was to make copies and
give them out. I was not yet sure to whom or how, so it
all seemed too much work because I was so busy with
my business and other things. Four days went by with
misery multiplying daily in my spirit. The fifth day,
during prayer time, the Lord gave me another important
message. Well, at this point, I could no longer ignore

His call to action. *"OK Lord, I'll do it or have no peace!"*
I prayed. Suddenly I felt wonderful **peace** coming over
me even before I stepped out in action to follow His
calling. All I had done was say, "Yes."

The next day I had five hundred copies of these four
pages printed. The next week I folded, mailed and
hand distributed some one hundred sets, but then I felt
I needed to have one thousand sets printed. I took the
four hundred I had already folded to the printer and
had them tab and mail out one thousand four hundred
sets to a zip code I chose. Now, I thought I was all
finished with the task the Lord had given me, but then
I began to hear in my heart that I was to send them
to the churches so that hopefully the pastors, priests,
and ministers would all realize the importance of God's
message and share it with their congregations. *Oh
brother, no rest,* I thought.

The next morning while walking at the park, unable
to shake the seed He planted in my heart two days

before, I decided I was **not** going to hesitate this time. *"Lord,"* I prayed, *"You said that we could ask You anything, believing, having no doubt and receive it. So Lord, I am asking You to tell me specifically what You want me to do when I get home after my prayer time. Whatever You tell me to do, I will do."*

Later, just as I had asked, the Holy Spirit told me clearly and specifically what to do. "Get two thousand sets printed to mail to churches and to be distributed in other ways." The next morning, still half asleep, the seeds of His plan were further planted in my heart and mind. These were to add Don Hunt's book, *"Pathway to God's Blessings"* and a letter to the four-page message being mailed. Then He proceeded to dictate to me what to put in the letter. I thought, *I wish I could remember this when I get up.* The words in the letter just kept playing over and over again, while I was trying to go back to sleep. I finally realized that I needed to get up and write them down. Sleep was not going to happen anyway. As usual, the words from the Holy Spirit were perfect.

A couple of days later, after work, the nine thousand pages were in the process of being printed, and I bought envelopes that the book would fit into easily. The Lord's plan was again in the works. It is hard to describe, but once I started, it was as if I were being encouraged, stimulated, and energized to accomplish His will. I am sure the angels assist in our acts of obedience. I have to admit, all the hesitation I demonstrate when the Lord asks something of me is puzzling because I'm the happiest when I'm doing something I **know** the Lord **called** me to do. Most of the reason for my hesitating to follow Him is because Satan immediately tells me it's just my idea, that it's too hard, or that there is not enough time, etc. This last time though, I did not listen to him. I hope I will stay alert to his deceitfulness. By now, I should know how He operates.

The last part of this is remarkable too because it

further shows the way the Lord has already worked out the details of a task He gives us to do. I told my brother about all the Lord was having me do, including sending out his recently-published book. He immediately offered to help with the financing.

You see, our Lord always has a perfect plan when He asks something of us. We do not know and we do not need to know all the details of the operation. We just need to take the initiative, develop whatever seed He has planted in our hearts and minds, and then He will tell us more as we need to know the next step. It really and truly works that way. Since it is not our plan, how could we know all the steps and how they will work out.

More than anything, I am learning how my **obedience** immediately results in the miracle of divine grace flooding my entire being with joy, purpose, fulfillment and peace.

NOTE: The pages I speak of here, the powerful messages from the Holy Spirit, are available on the Lord's Web site. **(www.hiscompanionship.com)** Go to September 16 & 20, 2004. The Lord's words are so important for our families in this world today!

Take a Chance On Him

CHAPTER 32

"Dear Lord, please send us the person You want to have our motor home." This was our prayer and we also had put an ad in the newspaper. It did not take long and indeed this woman was the right one because she needed it for her planned long road trip. She gave us $27,000.00—the amount we asked. We had planned to spend this money on several things: a new roof, new energy efficient windows, an insulation upgrade for the whole house, new six-inch gutters, and a used truck for my husband.

Shortly after selling the motor home, I thought of tithing on this money, but then I remembered we had tithed on it already as we worked each week and tithed before making the payments. However, a strong peaceful prompting made me think the Lord wanted us to tithe anyway. I mentioned it to my husband, and he voiced the same concern. Therefore, I said, "Honey, you're the head of the house; you pray about it—asking the Lord what He wants us to do, and that's what we'll do." At the breakfast table the next morning, Hans said, "Here is what the Lord made clear to me. We are to give the $2,700.00 to six people" and he proceeded to list who and how much. I got on it right away, and the checks were in the mail.

Now, before this tithing came up, Hans a retired contractor, had already figured approximately how much we were going to need for the roof, gutters, insulation, windows and truck, so now we were going to be short. But, we reminded each other that when we obey a calling from the Lord, only goodness and wonderful blessings follow. Our Father knows our needs; He just wants to know if we **trust** Him enough to obey.

Staying well informed concerning construction projects, my husband was insuring that we got the most for
our money plus quality work from the estimates coming in. I kept reminding Hans to go look for a truck so
he would not be tied down when I'm using the car, but
he kept putting it off. I knew it was because he hated
to spend the money on himself. He knew he was going to be short quite a bit, but he trusted the Lord. I did
not want to take any out of savings, but I thought I was
going to have to. All the estimates were in; all the deals
were made, and we were just waiting for the workers to
get each project started. Hans stayed close and inspect-
ed the work that was being done; he was even up on the
roof, which I did not like. A few days later, he comment-
ed on what good deals we were getting, that the men on
each project were very professional, and that they knew
what they were doing. It was apparent that the Lord was
at work for us again!

To our amazement, one day in the mail, there was an envelope from the Internal Revenue with a check for $2,700.00. We could not believe it—the exact amount the Lord had asked us to give! We had paid in too much last year. In all the excitement of planning for these projects, we had forgotten all about it. I do not know how we both could have forgotten about such a sizable return, but maybe the Lord blocked it from our minds to see if we would follow Him in obedience.

Remember, we are in training here on earth to become Christ-like, and Christ would have **trusted** the Father completely, without reserve. We had enough to finish the projects and buy the truck the Lord picked out.

The Father just wants us to **trust** Him above all else, to see Him as our **source.** When we do, He will always miraculously take care of the outcome to our sweet advantage. If we give to Him, He will then give back abundantly to us, but more importantly, He will personally show us how **close to our daily lives He really is.**

Heavenly Deal

CHAPTER 33

Finally, my shopping was finished; I was heading home. The traffic was picking up, but I was approaching the intersection where I turn right toward a quieter area of town where I live. Before coming to the intersection, I thought maybe that would be a good time to just scout out for a truck for my husband because we sold our motor home and needed a second vehicle. Hans had been too busy to go look himself. But then I thought, *No way. I don't know anything about trucks—what to ask for, look for, or what my husband would want.* By the time I had to make a choice to go straight or turn, I felt such a peaceful strong prompting about looking. I said aloud to the Lord, "I want to remember this moment because I can tell You're compelling me to go look even though I don't want to, so I will do it."

Through the light straight ahead I went, thanking Jesus for whatever He was doing. All the dealerships are together in the area I was headed. The Lord put in my mind to drive through the lots first, looking for trucks with no sticker on the window because Hans just wanted a used truck and new vehicles would have stickers. Then, if I saw any, I would go up to the entrance and ask a salesman if he had any used small trucks, automatic, air, and low mileage. I spotted one in the first lot.

The salesman opened up the truck and when I looked inside it appeared brand new. The tires were new; the paint job looked as if it had just come off the assembly line; it had low mileage, automatic, air, and it was a small truck. On his business card, I asked him to write the make of the truck, the year, the mileage, and the asking price. Then, I proceeded on to the next

dealer. After five dealerships, I had four cards to take
home to show Hans. He looked at each one and said,
"This is the only one I'd be interested in, the Dodge
Dakota Sport."

About 2:00 PM, we drove over to look at the truck.
He loved it. At one point in his life, Hans sold new and
used cars and trucks so he knew the ins and outs of
the trade. This truck was two and half years old, with
its original warranty. It was a sport edition with dual
exhaust, fancy wheels, custom radio/CD system, dark
smoked windows with sun visor on the windshield,
new bed liner, and an engine modified for more power
by the original manufacturer. "This is a **late**-life-crisis
truck," Hans jokingly said.

I thought to myself, *If he buys this one, the first one
I saw, then that means the Holy Spirit literally led me by
the nose from that intersection of decision right to the truck
the Lord picked out and saved for my husband.* We had a
certain amount that we wanted to spend. The Lord and

Hans negotiated the price down a bit to where it was just right. **No coincidence!**

The miracle is that, if we keep Jesus in our thoughts and talk to Him throughout the day, we will be sensitive to the gentle prompting and wisdom from the Holy Spirit, which keeps us from making mistakes and from missing the Father's blessings.

We know the reason this happened. It is because Hans **surrendered** to the Lord, **trusting** that he would be happy with whatever the Lord wanted to give him. Hans knows how perfectly the Lord works things out, and he did not say, "I want this; I want that." Instead, he said, "Thy perfect will be done. Thank You for whatever You give me, Lord, and I **praise** You for Your faithfulness to us." **(S.T.P.—Surrender, Trust and Praise)**.

My husband received more than he desired. He really loves driving his little truck. He says "little" because, before the motor home, he had a one-ton diesel truck. It makes me feel so close to the Holy Spirit when I think of how it felt when He nudged me to go looking. At first, I thought it was just an idea I had and a bad one at that, so I said, "No." However, the prompting continued. It was strong but peaceful, and that **peacefulness** is what made me stop and recognize that—if I just obey—something might be about to happen. That is the best I can describe how it felt to be led directly to this miracle. *"Thank You so much, Father, for taking such good care of all our little needs and desires when we truly* **trust You,***"* I prayed.

James 4 : 5

"... The Spirit who dwells in us

yearns jealously."

James 4 : 8

"Draw near to God and He will

draw near to you."

Psalm 48 : 14

"For this is God,

Our God forever and ever;

He will be our guide

Even to death."

Dodged a Bullet

CHAPTER 34

On April 1, 2005, my husband and I were turning our king size mattress from head to foot. I was standing at the foot of the bed reaching over the footboard. I wasn't thinking, moved too fast, reached out away from me while lifting, and threw the mattress forcefully to the right. The next day, I started having pain in my left waist area and hip.

I tried stretching, ice packs, and heating pads, but nothing was helping. I went to the chiropractor on April 6th and 8th, but his treatments did not relieve the pain and it was getting worse. Now I was really getting concerned. I put electrode patches on the painful area while working in my salon, which transmitted a pulsating or thumping motion through the muscle. I needed to relax the muscle. I had to lie down during my break and all evening after work. As soon as I got up in the morning, I barely made it to the chair where the heat from the heating pad relaxed it enough to allow me to brush my teeth and put on some clothes. I could tell the muscle was getting tighter and tighter because the pain was getting worse. I had to cancel my appointments for Saturday the 9th because the gripping pain was in my hip and left buttocks area now. To eat meals, I carefully sat on the edge of the chair, keeping my leg as straight as possible, trying to avoid that muscle spasm.

Saturday and Sunday were horrible! I had to stay flat on my back in bed all the time, lying on a heating pad to lessen the pain. Sunday, I could not get up from a sitting position because putting pressure on my left leg caused the gripping muscle spasm and it didn't want to let go. I had to stand for about three minutes before I could move. While lying in bed, I spent the time reading the Scriptures that tell of all the times the Lord Jesus Christ healed people. Repeatedly, dear Jesus says in His word,

"...thy **faith** has healed you," "...because of your **faith**, you are healed." Then, I remembered how many times the Lord had told me to **thank** Him for the opportunity to go through trials. He said this would give me a chance to **trust** Him with **peace**, while **praising** Him for His miracle power at work in the situation, **knowing** that He was working it out for my **best**, so that is exactly what I did. **(S.T.P.— Surrender, Trust and Praise)**. From that point on, I had real genuine peace while lying there. I did not know what my future would be, but I was sure my Lord and Savior did. *"Thank You so much dear Jesus, for my **gift of faith**,"* I prayed. *"It is the most important part of my life and always has been."*

Monday April 11, I woke up with severe pain. I was confused about whom to call—my internist, a chiropractor, or the Bone & Joint Clinic. In so much pain, I didn't want to waste time going from doctor to doctor. Feeling very frustrated, I asked Jesus whom to call. Each time I started to call my internist, I just didn't feel sure; something stopped me. It was the Holy Spirit. Then, in my spirit, I was guided to know the Lord's will. Suddenly, it was clear what I should do. I was to call the Bone & Joint Clinic. I got an appointment two hours later and felt very peaceful and grateful to my sweet Jesus. *"Dear Lord, Your guidance is always the best for us if we would just stop to ask and listen,"* I prayed.

My husband put hot moist towels on me for twenty minutes to relax the muscle spasm. It really helped so I was able to get dressed. The Lord took care of me because the only time the muscle spasm came back was when I was getting into the car to lie down on the back seat, which slants a bit, so I guess my waist twisted. That gripping muscle spasm struck again! I kept saying, *"Thank You, Jesus! Thank You, Jesus!"* The muscle relaxed quickly, and I slowly sat straight up. With the electrodes going and two ice bags, I was able to get there. My husband drove slowly and carefully so as not to hit any bumps in the road. He takes such good care of me.

I filled out the papers in the car, and the nurse brought a wheel chair out for me so I would not have to walk those long hallways. The bone specialist was wonderful. He'd been there eleven years. He was thorough, very nice, and explained things clearly to me. He recommended that I have several x-rays taken, and gave me a cortisone shot. He gave me samples of a muscle relaxer to take at night, and a prescription for six days of cortisone tablets. After inspecting the x-rays, he said, "You have serious degenerative disks and spurs on your spine. You need to have an MRI." He scheduled me for the next morning, April 12th.

The morning of April 13th the doctor said, "The results of your MRI show that you need surgery. You need three disks and several spurs removed. I am going to plead your case with one of our surgeons to try to get this taken care of as soon as possible because you're in so much pain." He came back in about fifteen minutes with an appointment for the next day and another cortisone shot.

By April 14th the cortisone shots were really working; I was so much better. While being escorted to the room, we noticed a doctor studying x-rays in the hall. In a little while, that same doctor, the surgeon, came in and said, "I want to take some additional x-rays because the MRI did not show what the previous x-rays had indicated." Then in the same building, in the same x-ray room, with the same x-ray equipment as before, they took four more x-rays adding a couple new positions. I wondered what the Lord was doing, but I knew He was in control. After a time, the surgeon returned with the verdict.

He sat and stated, "You have **minor** degenerative disks which is **normal** for your age. I recommend physical therapy to strengthen your lower abdomen and back muscles." I just sat there, blown away! *What did he say?* I thought to myself. Then I said, "What do you mean? Don't I need surgery?" "No, no," he said, "you do not need surgery." "But, we were told that I would need to have three disks and several spurs removed immediately. Are you saying that I do not need surgery at all?" "Yes, you just need to build up your body strength and learn how to bend, stand, and pick up things properly. If you consistently do the exercises and discipline yourself to maneuver as the therapist recommends, you can live the rest of your life without back pain."

Oh my God, my husband and I were stunned! We knew the Lord would heal me, but we could not get over how fast He had removed this big boulder from our lives. Hans was already very tired from waiting on me for just the four or five days that I was at my worst and could do little for myself. He told me later that he had been preparing himself mentally for taking care of me extensively for six weeks after back surgery. Now, miraculously, we had dodged the bullet in a matter of a few seconds. The surgeon's words were like **grace** pouring from his lips. We knew the Lord, our sweet Savior, who promises in His word healing of all sorts, had just performed a wonderful miracle for us. My sweetheart and I were almost in a daze for three days. In a few seconds, our life was back to normal.

Back in the car now, I phoned the physical therapy office, and learned they could take me that very day in a couple of hours. I could have suffered a lot longer if the Lord had not moved me through the system as fast as He did, but He promises favor for those who **give their lives to Him** and **trust Him**. We were astonished how smoothly the Lord had worked all this out. On **Monday** I saw the doctor and had x-rays. On **Tuesday** I had an MRI. On **Wednesday** I got the results. On **Thursday** I saw the surgeon and went to my first physical therapy session. I returned to work in my salon on **Friday** and

Saturday. The surgeon had said to wait a week before going back to work, but I didn't because I felt so much better. After praying about it, I was at peace working only one and a half hours for a couple of days. Then resting the weekend, I worked two and a half hours a couple of days before going back to normal hours but using the advice I was learning at physical therapy.

"Oh my Lord, only You could have done this for us!" I prayed. *"You are so faithful, so true to Your word! If only we wouldn't doubt You! If only we would* **believe** *what You say deep, deep in our hearts! The key to receiving miracles is to keep our* **focus** *on You, to* **surrender***, to* **trust** *You, even* **thank** *You and* **praise** *You for what's going on—no matter how devastating it may be.* **(S.T.P.— Surrender, Trust, and Praise)**. *You are bigger than any problem we could ever have, and You look out for Your faithful chil-dren—***not perfect children** *but faithful children."*

Psalm 103: 1-3

"Bless the Lord, O my soul,

And all that is within me,

bless His holy name!

Bless the Lord, O my soul,

And forget not all His benefits:

Who forgives all your iniquities,

Who heals all your diseases..."

The Kingdom Life

CHAPTER 35

It was January 15th of 2006, when I had been down a little bit for a few days, which I hardly ever am. Usually, the only time I would feel low was when I was exhausted; this was different. I started wishing I could be somewhere like Key West, Florida, but it was so expensive, far away, and too hot—unless we went within a couple of weeks. Still, it was Sunday afternoon, and I could not get it out of my mind. I searched on the internet, exploring accommodations, and found that I was right. Everything was way too expensive. Even so, every hotel and B&B I found was booked up. I didn't even check the condominiums because I knew they would be out of our price range. At this point, I said,

"OK, Lord, I will forget about it." Before I started, I had asked Him to let me know clearly if it was His will for us to go or not. Things were not working out, so I knew this trip was not His will. I put it out of my mind.

Later that same day, the Holy Spirit reminded me that my surroundings had nothing to do with the way I felt. He reminded me that I had put my work on the miracle accounts on hold for two months and that **obedience** was how to get my **joy** back. I proceeded to delve into His work again and indeed, whatever that funk was, it was gone. Purpose, fulfillment, and peace returned!

After working fervently a couple of days, the Key West thought came back. However, this time I felt perfectly content to stay home. I was not down at all. The thought just came into my mind to get the materials I had saved from my last trip there a few years before. I found that I had a booklet, which listed all the accommodations in Key West with pictures, descriptions,

locations on a map, and prices. I didn't realize I had
it. So, I decided to call some of them to see if any were
more reasonable or even available around February
1st. Of course, I prayed and asked the Lord not to let
me waste much time on this, if it were not His will, but
I had a peaceful calm about it. I made several calls.
To my surprise, Victorian homes converted into condominiums, in great locations, and at unpredictably
reasonable prices, narrowed the search down to two.
I then went to the internet to see them and asked the
Lord to let me know which one. Only one would come
up, so I took that as a sign. *"Thank You, Jesus!"*
I prayed.

   I had begun checking the internet for airfare and a
rental car when I realized the prices were excessively
high, but I said, "Lord, thank You for getting us a better price, if this is Your will." I really wanted to listen
to His voice in my heart so I would not miss His will.
I was not going if there was any doubt. I kept look-

ing. After searching a short while, I secured a flight and rental car at a great price. I knew this was the Lord's will because I had **perfect peace**. If in the back of my mind I had been thinking that I really should not be doing this or I hope this is the right thing to do, I would have **known** this was the Lord saying, "No, this is not My will for you at this time!"

On the contrary, when the trip was all set up, I realized that it had been orchestrated by the guidance of the Holy Spirit because it all went so smoothly. He also reminded me that it had all started to evolve, after I had put **His work first** by laying the Key West desire down and picking up the miracle accounts, and working on them for two solid days. Of course, I continued to make the Lord's work a priority while carrying in my heart that awesome feeling of His closeness. Jesus responded so quickly to the desire of my heart when I decided to focus on Him above all else! He is remarkable! We left on January 31st for two weeks. The house the Lord gave us was great! We loved it! The weather was in the mid-seventies. The trip was very relaxing. We marvel at how life is so much easier when we let Jesus do the planning.

When we deny self, our personal desires, to give ourselves totally to our Father and Creator, Lord and Savior, Holy Spirit and teacher, we can never lose! When we take one step in obedience toward Him, He takes one hundred steps of love toward us. When we give one inch, He gives one hundred miles.

The miracle here is that I could see again the way the Holy Spirit was teaching me about the priorities of the Kingdom life. Our Father promises to give us all of our hearts' desires, but in the Kingdom life our will takes a back seat to His. We must put His will first! However, peace and joy accompany us on the journey to bold and beautiful rewards, even here on this earth.

Psalm 37:4

"Delight yourself in the Lord,

And He shall give you the desires

of your heart."

Reality of Miracles

CHAPTER 36

Inspired by the Holy Spirit during my prayer time

"I am all that is needed, and I am waiting to give miracles to **all** My children. The problem is they do not really believe. To receive a miracle in your life, you **must believe!** This is the catalyst, the spark that ignites the release of a miracle. The very nature of a miracle is that it is **believed before** it is seen. (Matthew 13:58 NKJV) says, 'Now, He (Jesus) did not do many mighty works there because of their unbelief.' Dear children, when will you realize the significance of **faith?**

"I cannot shower My blessings on those who do not even know Me well enough to recognize them. How

---

would that bring glory to My Father? No, the **purpose** of miracles is to edify the body of Christ and enlighten people as to the power of the creator of **all**. Miracles are a manifestation of My love. Miracles prove My power, My glory and My truth.

"Give Me your life so I can demonstrate this super-natural phenomenon for you. Give Me your heart, soul, and mind. Get to know Me through prayer and reading My word. Trust Me with your life no matter what comes at you along the way. I will show you divine miraculous loving power that reaches beyond the understanding of man. I want this for **all** of you, but you **must believe!**"

NOTE: For more inspired words from our loving Lord, Savior and Friend, through the power of the Holy Spirit, go to His Web site. **(www.hiscompanionship.com)**

Can You Expect Miracles?

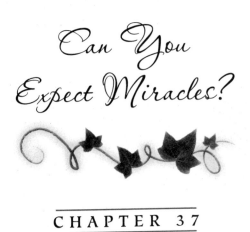

CHAPTER 37

Inspired by the Holy Spirit during my prayer time

"Dear children, My promises are not just words. If you **believe** in Me, if you **know** Me, if you trust what I have promised, then **YOU** can **expect** miracles. When problems arise, let your heart be full of joy because I have given you another opportunity to see My miracle power at work and My holy promises fulfilled in truth.

"Dear children, you must not fear anything when I live inside you, when you have given Me domain over your very existence. I am your Father, after all. Do you think I would let harm come to you when you **call**

on Me to help you, to lead you, to heal you? No, that will never happen! I am your rock, your grounding rod when life throws you a tumultuous situation.

"**Hold onto Me!** Look to see what I say in Scripture. **Hold on** with **total trust** having **no doubt**, and then, **surrender** with fullness of heartfelt joy, with **praise** pouring from your heart, mind, and lips. Never have fear; **you know who your Father is!** Keep your eyes on His love and glory. **Peace** will keep you strong and joyful."

NOTE: For more inspired words from our loving Lord, Savior and Friend, through the power of the Holy Spirit, go to His Web site. (**www.hiscompanionship.com**)

Matthew 10: 20

"For it is not you who speaks, but the spirit of your Father who speaks in you."

Peace in Times of Trouble... S.T.P.

CHAPTER 38

Inspired by the Holy Spirit during my prayer time

1.) Give your life to JESUS—SURRENDER all.

2.) ASK FORGIVENESS for past grievances against God.

3.) FORGIVE anyone you might hold a grudge against—anyone you think ill of.

4.) LET GO of all that could possibly stand between you and the wonderful PEACE God has for you.

The HOLY SPIRIT will then watch over you, guide

you, and give you PEACE and JOY that only comes from God.

WHEN TROUBLE HITS.....USE S.T.P.

"S"..... SURRENDER:

Take the sad, hurting, or worrisome feeling, person, or thing and lift your hands to Heaven giving it to Jesus. SURRENDER it completely to Him.

"T"..... TRUST:

Because you TRUST that Jesus: a) loves you so much and b) proved it by dying on the cross for your sins, that you can be with Him for all ETERNITY, now you can know He will NOT LET anything happen to you which is not in HIS PERFECT PLAN for your life. Therefore...

"P"..... PRAISE:

PRAISE JESUS and THANK HIM for His love and care for you each and every time the problem presents itself. JESUS will handle the problem, and you will have HIS HEAVENLY PEACE.

GOD the FATHER never said that on this earth we would not have troubles and sorrows, but He gave us **HIS SON, JESUS,** to **die for our sins,** to give us a chance for **EVERLASTING LIFE IN HEAVEN.**

And when we **give our life** to JESUS CHRIST, the HOLY SPIRIT comes to **live in our hearts** to give us PEACE, to GUIDE, to PROTECT, and to help us BECOME more and more **like** JESUS during our lifetime.

Read a little bit of the **BIBLE** each day and give Him some quiet time, then the **HOLY SPIRIT** can **TEACH** you more about **JESUS** and **HIS PEACE will fill your being.**

NOTE: STP is covered in detail in *"Pathway to God's Blessings"* by Don Hunt, Light of the World Publishing.

Matthew 10: 27

"Whatever I tell you in the dark,

speak in the light; and

Whatever you hear in the ear,

preach on the housetops."

My Favorite Lifelong Prayers

CHAPTER 39

Oh my Jesus, I love You and for love of You, I repent of all my sins. My heart longs for You. Come and take possession of it forever.

Angel of God, my guardian dear, to whom God's Love commits thee here, ever this day and night be at my side to light and guard, to rule and guide. Amen.

A Note from the Author

Mary Hunt Dewitz

"Please visit my Web site **(www.hiscompanionship.**

com) *where I have for the last ten years recorded inspired words from the Lord during prayer time. The Lord wants each of us to join Him in the secret place of our heart. When we read and contemplate His Holy Word and then remain still, quiet and open, yes, the Lord will speak to us through the Holy Spirit living in our heart. Most of us are too distracted with the pressures, pleasures and desires promoted by the world. Therefore, we may not have experienced this closeness that our Lord and Savior wants with us.*

"Pure worship is the most desired frame of mind that invites the infilling of God's loving gentle voice. He indeed will speak directly to us, each of us, if we seek Him by spending time alone with Him in His Word, in His presence, desiring above all His will in our lives. At times the discipline it takes to sit quietly before Him is difficult, but immensely worth it."

My Prayer to the Lord

Holy Spirit, tell me what to say to people who are suffering, when they ask, "Where is my miracle?"
In my spirit I heard this:

- "Seek me above all else.

- Desire to live according to My will for your life.

- Know what I promise in My Word.

- Believe what I promise.

- Surrender your situation...

    suffering, uncertainty, needs.

- Trust My love for you completely.

- Spend your time praising me for My perfect plan rather than looking or dwelling on the problem at hand.

- Keep your focus on Me and My Word.

- Joyfully anticipate witnessing My miracle power released into your situation.

YOU WILL SEE IT EVERY TIME!"

Jesus Christ Loves You and Will Never Give Up On You

No matter what you do to yourself, to your loved ones, to your enemies, Jesus Christ loves you and will never give up on you.

His love is always reaching out to you. All you must do to receive this Love is to accept His Love. Say this now, say it out loud if possible. "Thank you Jesus. I accept your Love. I accept your will for my life."

Jesus Christ died for your sins and thereby gave you eternal life. Now tell our Lord you accept His free gift of eternal life and surrender your will to His will.

All through the day repeat over and over "Thank you Jesus," and Jesus will give you inner peace that will surpass your most cherished earthly dreams.

Jesus Christ is alive today and the Bible is "The Word". Admit your needs, accept Him into your life and change your world. Read the word of God daily and learn the truth.

Jim Hunt,
Chairman
Hunt Brothers Pizza Company, LLC
email: jim@lightoftheworldpublishing.com

THE PATHWAY SERIES

Book One

Don Hunt

Common Sense For America
It's Not About Change. It's About Choice!

Right Choices
Produce Right Change
We must return to the basic principles of liberty and justice that made America great. The Illustrations and stories will set a fire in your heart as you read Don's common sense solutions for twenty of our greatest problems we face today.

246 easy to read pages

Book Two

Don Hunt

Pathway to God's Blessings
How to get in a position where God is free to Bless You

The Secret to An Abundant Life
Using many illustrations and stories that have occurred in his own life, Don will lead you down the pathway we must follow in order to get in a position where God can bless you. Don says this position is the Secret to "The Abundant Life".

161 easy to read pages

These books, as well as the special "United We Stand" flag stickers and Common Sense for America brochures may be purchased at your local book store or online from:
www.lightoftheworldpublishing.com

THE PATHWAY SERIES

Book Three

Mary Hunt
Dewitz

Miracles Along the Path
My Personal Testimonies
Spanning 50 Years

Do miracles really happen?
Yes! Mary tells of her personal experiences with miracles spanning 50 years. Come along on this journey to realize what God can do for you in your life today.

217 easy to read pages

Book Four

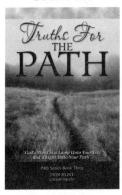

Don Hunt

Truths for the Path
God's Word is a Lamp Unto Your Feet
and a Light Unto Your Path

By means of stories and child-like illustrations, Don guides, encourages and motivates the reader to a deeper level of spiritual maturity. This is a great book for group discussion or Bible study. This information will help you avoid the pitfalls along the path to the abundant life.

312 easy to read pages

These publications and other materials can be viewed and previewed on our web site.
www.lightoftheworldpublishing.com

About the Author
M a r y   H u n t   D e w i t z

Mary lives in Franklin, Tennessee and has been married for 29 years. She became a Catholic nun, but felt called to leave after a couple of years. Continuing her education in teaching and business, she eventually found her niche in hair design and opened her own business nineteen years ago.

At the age of fifty-one, the Lord led Mary to write down the miracles that have happened in her life. The miracles cover a span of fifty years, eight to fifty-eight, which show how attentive the Lord is to the details of His children's lives, when we call on Him in faith and trust.